90 Daily Devotions

GRIT

GOD'S WAY

Break the cycle of burnout, hone your holy hustle, and get ready to rise up and run in your purpose with confidence!

Written by
Heather Wallace

To my loving husband, Chris. Thank you for believing in me long before I believed in myself. You are my biggest cheerleader, steadiest support, and constant love.
I love you most.

To my beautiful children, Joshua and Jocelin. I love you both more than you could ever imagine. My greatest gift and most adored accomplishment will always be that of being your mama.
You make me so proud!

Welcome

Before you begin this 90 day journey, you may also want to purchase Heather's 90 day journal as a companion!

It is a powerful 90-day journal with a prompted daily outline to develop GRIT God's Way!

Establish a structured a.m. and p.m. routine to create and develop biblical mindsets, habits, and disciplines that will enable you to win each day!

Scan the QR code below to get your copy today!

You will find two cover styles, both containing the same great content!

Day 1

What is GRIT and how do I get it?

Lean in, friend, because I've got a word for you today that'll light a fire under your soul! Now listen, you all know I'm a massive fan of grit. Heck, I teach it! But let me tell you, there's grit, and then there's God-Graced Grit!

There's a Rhythm of Grace, a divine tempo that's tailored just for the race you're in.

Look, I get it. Life is a battlefield, and sometimes that warrior spirit in you can feel more weary than warrior-like. You're hustling but it feels hollow, am I right? But here's the game-changer: Holy Hustle!

That's right, when your grind is God-ordained, let me tell you, friend, you're unstoppable!
It's not about muscling through on your strength.

It's about tapping into a strength that is greater, higher, and infinite!

It's about aligning your passion, your dream, your unique calling with the grace of God.

You see, when you blend hustle with holiness, you get a match made in heaven—a power-packed combo that's more energizing than a double espresso!

So, what's the strategy, you ask? Simple. Step one, take your weary soul to the wellspring of life—God Himself. Let Him refresh you, renew you, and give you a divine perspective on your assignment, your calling, your dream. Step two, recommit to that dream with a God-graced grit that can tear down any obstacle, leap over any wall, and bring your God-given vision to life.

Hold onto your hats, because when you understand the rhythm of God's grace for your race, you'll not only regain your peace and strength, but you'll be propelled into a purpose-driven life that'll set your soul ablaze!

"But the people that do know their God shall be strong, and do exploits."
Daniel 11:32 KJV

Do you ever feel like life is racing by at warp speed and everything and anything is being thrown your way??

I couldn't count the times I have felt this. You take the step of faith and instead of being met with instant breakthrough, healing, provision, or promotion, you are hit with obstacles, resistance, sickness, and unexpected circumstances.

I see you, friend. I hear you. Anxiety surfaces. Fear rises. Worry consumes.

Overwhelm has set in and you feel like hiding until the storm passes. But what if we use the other definition of overwhelm?

I'm not an English major, but I love that overwhelm is a verb! It's an action word. It is not a state of being. I don't have to fall victim to being something. Instead I can get into action and do something!

One definition of overwhelm means to OVERCOME!

Overcome fear with faith.
Overcome anxiety with expectation.
Overcome worry with worship.

Set your mind on the things above. Use your words to agree and declare His word. Shift your thoughts, shift your vision and your voice, and you will shift your future!

Instead of waiting until you feel your way into action. Try acting your way into feeling!

"Keep your thoughts continually fixed on all that is authentic and real, honorable and admirable, beautiful and respectful, pure and holy, merciful and kind. And fasten your thoughts on every glorious work of God, praising him always."
Philippians 4:8 TPT

Whose approval are you seeking?

You don't need anyone else's approval to be who God called you to be!

I don't know who "they" are in your life. But hear this! They aren't accountable for what God has placed in your heart. You are! It may be unconventional. It may be unpopular. It may not be the "societal norm." Last I checked, Jesus disrupted all kinds of doctrine and thought processes. That's the example we have.

Say yes anyway! Pursue your purpose despite their opinions.

Maybe you don't agree with everyone's methods, but we can all celebrate when lives are changed. Maybe you don't jive with everyone's delivery style, but you can't discount the message. Maybe you don't agree with everyone's tactics, but you can't argue with love.

Decide today, "I am pressing on, unwavering, unashamed, and in relentless pursuit of sharing hope with all who will hear."

May the women around me and the ones coming behind me believe that they can do more than they dream. May our daughters know that they are handcrafted, chosen, called, and equipped for greatness. May they refuse to shrink to make others comfortable.

Hey friend, preach the gospel, share your story, build that business, and clap for those who won't clap for you! This is kingdom. We all have a place here!

"And so it is in the body of Christ. For though we are many, we've all been mingled into one body in Christ. This means that we are all vitally joined to one another, with each contributing to the others. God's marvelous grace imparts to each one of us varying gifts..."
Romans 12:5-6 TPT

I hear the Lord say:

This is the time I am repositioning my sons and daughters. Those who have been sleeping on their gifts are being woken up and activated. The things they have only tasted in small portions in the past are being activated for this season. What felt like only a tease of my promise was but a taste of what was to come and now is. The testing and trying of this last season was to put faithfulness on display. I am calling my children to demolish the idols, both entitlement and earning.

It was never about earning. It was about LEARNING.

Testing reveals the gap in learning. It is never to degrade or put to shame. That is the enemy's playground. I am a good teacher who takes my students under my wing. When necessary, I have withdrawn you from the presence of others to tutor you in private.

Perhaps it has felt like punishment, but I am telling you it was only private preparation.

Day 4

The time has come and now is. Step back out. You will do it differently now. You have learned so much and are ready for the next. Go in faith, not fear. Trust, not timidity.

Courage, not cowardice. I am with you. I have prepared you. I am faithful to my promise. And you have been faithful to your process.

Sleeping Giants are being awakened in my sons and daughters. Go now under the sound of my voice in power and authority into your next field of purpose!

"Rise up in splendor and be radiant, for your light has dawned, and Yahweh's glory now streams from you! Look carefully! Darkness blankets the earth, and thick gloom covers the nations, but Yahweh arises upon you and the brightness of his glory appears over you! Nations will be attracted to your radiant light and kings to the sunrise-glory of your new day."
Isaiah 60:1-3 TPT

Is your heart weary?

You are seen, and you are loved. Fully and completely just as you are!

I know you're hurting inwardly and smiling outwardly. I know you secretly feel embarrassed and ashamed. I know your anxiety is crippling you, and depression is trying to silence you.

You are great at hiding it, but I know this isn't what you thought life would look like. I know you really want to be excited and energetic. I know you want to be the fun, fully present person you've always dreamed of being.

I know you really want to stop feeling like a fraud and a failure. I know you want to step into rooms like God hand-delivered the invitation for you!

Your time is coming.

○○○ strong, patient & happy marriage

It will feel scary. It won't feel sure. You won't know that you can do it. You'll only have a spoonful of hope. But sweet friend, that's all you need to take the next step. *self help*

Soon, this pain will become your purpose. Soon, you'll thrive again! Your best days are not behind you. They are ahead. And this struggle will soon become your story that will serve the world.

Take the leap today! Do it afraid! If you don't quit, you won't fail!

If Peter can step out of his boat in the midst of a raging storm, imagine what you can do!

"Then Peter got down out of the boat, walked on the water and came toward Jesus. But when he saw the wind, he was afraid and, beginning to sink, cried out, "Lord, save me!" Immediately Jesus reached out his hand and caught him."
Matthew 14:19-21 NIV

Day 6

If I could give you one gift today, it would be to know this...

You. Are. Enough!!!

I spent so many years of my life feeling so unworthy, incapable, unqualified, and undervalued. I strived to become enough.

I so deeply wanted to serve and have my life make a difference. I sacrificed so much trying to become enough for others whom I would never be enough for. Yet, for some, I am too much. Go figure. You'll never please them all. So find your tribe and live to please an audience of one!

Today, I am a little older and a little wiser. The only person I strive to become is the best version of the one God uniquely created as me!

I can rest in knowing I am enough because God in me is enough. When I discovered that truth and embraced it, it became the catalyst to the freedom I needed.

Not only to live out my own purpose and passions but to begin to awaken others to their potential and give them permission to pursue their own! God's grace is enough, and his power is sufficient in our insufficiency.

This world needs YOU! Strong, capable, passionate, brave, and ready! Not perfect. Not arrived. Not put together. But pursuing!

I pray that today this stirs your heart and causes you to embrace your destiny. You were created for more, and you, my friend, are ENOUGH!!!

What would today look like if you dared to believe this is true? How would you show up differently?

"But he answered me, "My grace is always more than enough for you, and my power finds its full expression through your weakness." So I will celebrate my weaknesses, for when I'm weak, I sense more deeply the mighty power of Christ living in me."
2 Corinthians 12:9 TPT

Have you ever prayed and only heard silence?

"People pray for cake. But when the almighty gives them eggs, flour, butter, a pan and an oven, they get frustrated and leave the kitchen." - Unknown

Praying means partnering with God. This is not an excuse to sit back and do nothing. It is an encouragement from our Father to be diligent and dedicated to moving forward in our purpose and getting into action so that He can take our efforts and create something for His glory!

When the disciples needed money to pay taxes, Jesus could have just handed over a coin. Instead, He partnered with them and sent them to put their hands to work and go fishing. It was in their doing that the miracle manifested.
Faith is powerful! But faith without works is dead. More often than not, the miracle is preceded by obedience and the obedience is found in action!

Active faith demands participation.

Truths to remember and declare today:

1. I am never alone!
2. The ingredients in my hands are more than enough for what God wants me to create.
3. Prayer works! But the answers rarely come in the form we think they will.
4. I might sometimes get frustrated, but I refuse to leave the kitchen! He is working with me to make ALL things beautiful in their time.

Where does your faith require action and obedience to become full and complete?

"But someone will say, "You have faith. I do good works." Show me your faith that doesn't do good works. And I will show you my faith by what I do."
James 2:18 NIRV

What mountain are you facing today? Name it!

"Perhaps you have been assigned this mountain to show others that it can be moved!" -Unknown

The struggle is real!!! But so is your soon-coming story of victory! It's hard to see and know the seed in the season when your vision is obscured by the storm of your circumstances. But the next season will reveal the seed for what it was.

In every season of hardship came the seed of future success. Only at the time, I didn't know.

I didn't know depression held the seed of empathy.
I didn't know poverty held the seed of generosity.
I didn't know insecurity held the seed of empowerment.
I didn't know obesity held the seed of transformational inspiration.
I didn't know suffering held the seed of success.
I didn't know obscurity held the seed of the stages I now stand on.

I didn't know the *hard times were only preparation for the prayers long prayed.*

Here I stand, screaming with my whole heart, beckoning you to press on! If only you could see the beautiful bright future that awaits you and the impact of your voice and your story!

You may not understand it now, and you don't have to like it. But within the seed of your suffering is the preparation of your prayers.

This is your moment! How will you choose to embrace it?

"Then Mordecai told them to reply to Esther, 'Do not imagine that you in the king's palace can escape any more than all the Jews. For if you remain silent at this time, relief and deliverance will arise for the Jews from another place and you and your father's house will perish. And who knows whether you have not attained royalty for such a time as this?"
Esther 4:13-14 NASB

Day 9

"Do not fear!" But what about when I feel afraid?

That statement is found 365 times throughout the world of God! I don't believe that's a coincidence. One for each day of the year. It's a daily command.

But here's the thing. I often feel afraid. Afraid to take the next step. Afraid to let go. Afraid to hold on. Afraid I'll mess it up. Afraid I'll take the wrong step. Afraid of what others may think. And on and on. But that's not what the Bible means.

The Bible never says I won't feel afraid; it commands me not to fear.

How can that be?

Did you know that fear is a verb? It's an action word. Faith is a noun… it's something we have. It is a thing we possess as believers. Afraid is also a noun. It is a feeling you can have.

But fear is a verb. It is an action. Which means it is something I can choose not to do or participate in. That doesn't mean I won't have the feeling. I may feel afraid, but I don't have to partner with it and act in fear!

Regardless of the feeling, I choose to ACT in Faith!

You can actively pursue your future with faith, or you can actively pursue and live out your fear. But make no mistake; it is a choice.

So do the scary things. Feel afraid and do it anyway. You possess faith already!

Walk in it. Use it. And know that God is with you wherever you go!

"So do not fear, for I am with you; do not be dismayed, for I am your God. I will strengthen you and help you;
I will uphold you with my righteous right hand."
Isaiah 41:10 NIV

What is pain producing in your life?

So often, I have been so guilty of avoiding difficult or challenging moments or seasons. I don't like even the thought or idea of possible failure. And who in the world likes hard or painful times? Certainly not me.

But I have been on an intentional journey to grow and develop myself. As a leader, I have determined to lead myself first. It was significant progress for me to go from avoiding pain or challenges to enduring them. I'm just being honest. It was real progress.

But I am in a season now where I choose to move from enduring to embracing. The truth is those moments, seasons, circumstances, or the likes are usually the very things that create the most momentum and progress forward in my own life. It is usually in those times when I see the hand of God move in ways I might otherwise miss.

I have decided to embrace them and hold them close with a different expectation for the outcome.

I will be better for it, I will learn from it, and God will be glorified in it.

I will slow down enough to respond and resist the urge to react without intention.

But be careful. Sometimes the temptation is to stay in a season too long or allow a season to become an identity. Seasons will change. So if you find yourself in the midst of winter, don't be afraid to start looking for signs of spring. It's coming!!!

For it all, I will say, "Thank you!"

"Consider it pure joy, my brothers and sisters, whenever you face trials of many kinds, because you know that the testing of your faith produces perseverance. Let perseverance finish its work so that you may be mature and complete, not lacking anything."
James 1:2-4 NIV

Day 11

Do you ever have those days that require that extra cup of coffee?

But really, what can we do when we have "those days?" You know the ones…

When our schedules get messed up with unexpected hiccups

Pivot and embrace the adventure. Take some deep breaths, and remember, if you can't control it, it shouldn't control you!

When we feel there's more task list than time

Focus on what's most important. Will it matter 5 years from now?

When tensions arise in our relationships

Seek to understand over being understood. Take ownership. Be the first to apologize.

When life feels unfair, and we find ourselves in circumstances, we would never choose look around.

Look for the opportunity in the obstacle. Instead of navigating around it, draw from it as you move through it. That obstacle can be an assassin or a teacher. You decide. Will you become a victim or a student?

I'm no expert in any of these areas yet! But you better believe I am in pursuit! Give yourself permission to pursue better without the pressure of perfection!!

"Lean on, trust in, and be confident in the Lord with all your heart and mind and do not rely on your own insight or understanding.
In all your ways know, recognize, and acknowledge Him, and He will direct and make straight and plain your paths."
Proverbs 3:5-6 AMPC

How do you manage disappointment?

I didn't pick this place or this pace. But I am taking so much comfort in the assurance that even these steps I didn't pick or anticipate are ordered by the author of my story. I'm expectant for how this season will be woven together with the days I haven't experienced yet for my good and for His glory. Because, above all, I believe He is working all things for my good.

Maybe you're managing some disappointment today or some unforeseen circumstances.

You can cry, but you can't quit.

You can bring your disappointment and struggles to your Father with honesty and vulnerability but receive His strength, love, and grace and move forward. There are some promises for you!

He is near to the brokenhearted.

He gives beauty for ashes and joy for sorrow. Daybreak will always follow the darkness, and this, too, shall pass.

Nothing will be wasted, and perhaps this will be the greatest catalyst for what is coming. Look for those glimpses of His glory, and know you are not alone.

He is working in your waiting. And He can do far more than you could ask, think, or imagine. What if this prepares you for a "next" season that is far greater?

Trust Him. Trust the process. And keep your hearts and minds anchored in truth!

"And we know that God causes everything to work together for the good of those who love God and are called according to his purpose for them."
Romans 8:28 NLT

How do you make your moments count?

One day we will draw our last breath here on earth and our next in eternity. There, I believe we will get this incredible chance to look back and see all the lives we've impacted. I mean, every single one, can you imagine? My prayer is that every single day I will be able to lengthen that line!

Not too many years ago, things got really interesting. I decided to take this huge leap of faith and shake up my whole life by stepping into a new field of ministry that looked rather unconventional at the time. And let me tell you, not everyone around me was totally on board with my plan back then. But you know what's great? I live for the applause and approval of one!

Divine invitations often come disguised in some of the most unexpected opportunities.

Yep, those doors you've prayed for? Well, they might show up in disguises you'd never think of. It's like God's saying, "Hey, I've got something awesome in store for you!"

Turns out, the path to those amazing opportunities might look a little different from what we expect, but that's where the magic happens.

So, here's my friendly advice for you: **Embrace those unexpected twists and turns that life throws your way.** You never know when they will lead you right to the blessings you've been dreaming about. And let's keep adding to the lives we're impacting, day by day. You being authentically and unapologetically you will change the world! Your voice and your story matters! Who knew our stories could turn out this inspiring, huh?

Keep shining, and trust that those detours might just be leading you to some seriously awesome destinations.

"See, I am doing a new thing! Now it springs up; do you not perceive it? I am making a way in the wilderness and streams in the wasteland."
Isaiah 43:19 NIV

Grace & Gratitude. For her. For the woman I once was.

**Can you look back on your life and embrace both?
Today I choose to give myself grace.**

Grace for the woman who was so very sick. Grace for the surgery she didn't plan that sent her body into menopause with no warning and no hormone replacement. Grace for the season of loss and grief. Grace for the depression she battled. Grace for the illnesses her body would suffer. Grace for the months she simply survived. Grace for the time she couldn't be the wife, mother, or woman she so desired to be. Grace for the season she spent feeling trapped in a body she didn't recognize. Grace for the life she would forfeit while she recovered. Grace for the journey it would require her to get there.

And Gratitude.
Gratitude for the God who healed her. Gratitude for the second chance. Gratitude for the lessons learned. Gratitude for those who loved her at her lowest. Gratitude when what could have been an excuse to complain became the fuel to contend. Gratitude that yesterday doesn't define tomorrow.

Gratitude that great pain produces great purpose. Gratitude that she quit allowing other people's opinions to hold her hostage, and she found freedom to live the life she was created for. Gratitude that the war she fought for her own freedom would one day become the battle plan for freeing others. Gratitude that He who is within her was FAR GREATER than he who would oppose her.

And now- GRIT! Grit to press on. Grit to persevere. Grit to not settle. Grit to continue. Grit to contend. Grit to unlock the prison doors of others with compassion. Grit to give hope even when that is unpopular. Grit to stand boldly in the face of adversity!!!!

What can you look back on with both grace and gratitude for yourself today?

"But he said to me, "My grace is sufficient for you, for my power is made perfect in weakness." Therefore I will boast all the more gladly of my weaknesses, so that the power of Christ may rest upon me."
2 Corinthians 12:9 ESV

I want you to quit! Right this minute.

No, I don't say that often so listen closely. What most people don't realize is you can do ANYTHING if you quit one thing- being chicken.

Let me tell you what chickens do…they spend their ENTIRE life pecking at the ground for food. Chickens move from thing to thing, pecking the ground only for the small portions laying at their feet. They never leave the ground. They don't lift their eyes to look further ahead. They live their lives settling only for what someone else chose to scatter at their feet.

You, my friend, were created to be an eagle!

Eagles have a different perspective. Eagles take flight. They leave the comfort of the ground and soar above their current circumstances to look miles ahead. They look for the best options. They make a calculated plan on how to achieve what they see from a different perspective. You'll never settle when you choose to soar because you've been exposed to the possibilities of more.

QUIT being a chicken! If you spend your whole life settling for the scraps at your feet, you will miss out on a whole other life you could be creating.

What do you want the future to hold?

Answer that question and then make a change because we all will be accountable for what we do with our one and only life.

Today is the perfect time to make a change. Are you in a major rut? Do you find yourself settling or soaring?

Make a decision today to rise up!

"Those who entwine their hearts with Yahweh will experience divine strength. They will rise up on soaring wings and fly like eagles, run their race without growing weary, and walk through life without giving up."
Isaiah 40:31 TPT

What can you control??

I talk a lot about transitions, shifting, and the unexpected paths we experience in this journey of life because... well, I have found it to be familiar territory in many seasons of my own.

So what can you control?? You! Your response. Your expectation. Your outlook. Your attitude. Although you may not have picked this path, you can wholeheartedly trust the one who picked it for you.

You can look at all the things you have given up to take the step of obedience, or you can look at all the things you have gained by taking it.

I coach hundreds of people on a weekly basis and empower them to make bold moves, take faith steps, take ownership and responsibility, and become the best version of themselves to live this one and only life to the full! I believe freedom is rarely given but often fought for and forged with determination, community, faith & grit. I watch people do it day in and day out in every area of life!

Day 16

I watch generational curses shatter and the trajectory of entire families shift because one person made a decision and committed to the process.

But what about the curve balls or the course corrections? What about the unexpected turns you didn't choose or even anticipate? You can't control everything in life. And that feeling of being out of control is often the greatest gateway to frustration and anxiety.

I am hereby giving you bold permission to change your perspective! You already know I'm a word girl and surround myself with life-speaking sayings. I bought a sign for my bedroom one year ago that says, "What is coming is far better than what is gone." Maybe you don't see it yet but dare to believe it. Embrace the season you're in and the unexpected with great expectation!

"A man without self-control is like a city broken into and left without walls."
Proverbs 25:28 ESV

"We can't both want growth and question God when we get growing pains." -Ashley Jackson

It's time to embrace the growing pains! We pray for so much but get frustrated and, dare I say, even a little bitter when God begins to stretch us to enlarge our capacity enough to hold all that we have prayed for. Can I help prepare you and set your expectations a little?

The bigger the dream, the bigger the desire, the bigger the calling, the bigger the impact... the greater the stretching. The greater the stretching, the greater the growing pains.

When you know what to expect, the painful season isn't as scary because you know what is awaiting you on the other side. Mamas, do you remember the stretching and the pain of bringing another life into this world? Our bodies grew in capacity to hold the promise of what we prayed for. Birthing pains don't create fear or anxiety because we know it is necessary for the process of our promise.

Perhaps you haven't experienced that for yourself. Perhaps that is a promise you are still praying for or a place of unfamiliarity. Can you then recall the days when your body grew as a child and into a young adult? I used to get the worst leg cramps. What felt like pain was actually preparation. I'm now 5'7" and quite grateful for the stretching season. And though the nights of pain were long, the years of growth were short. And those short years have given me the height I will walk in from now on. The greater the pain, the greater the capacity!

Here is your spiritual "what to expect when expecting" encouragement for the day. Don't let the pain of change, resistance, or obstacles surprise or scare you! Let it instead encourage your heart that the birthing time is right around the corner and holding your promise will be worth the pain!

"Increase is coming, so enlarge your tent and add extensions to your dwelling. Hold nothing back! Make the tent ropes longer and the pegs stronger. You will increase and spread out in every direction. Your sons and daughters will conquer nations and revitalize desolate cities."
Isaiah 54:2-3 TPT

Don't wait on the feeling before you take action!

Here's a little insight for you...

The feeling you had when you made that decision and commitment will RARELY be the same feeling you have when it's time to create and carry it out!

Feelings and emotions are fickle. They change often. Instead of letting them lead you, you take charge and lead them. You have what it takes!

What I feel like doing and what I need to do seem to rarely line up.

But what I have discovered is that as I get about the Father's business and creating the life I believe I am capable of, the feelings somehow tend to catch up! The strength is within you to do what you need to do; that is the promise of God!

So if you woke up today feeling overwhelmed, anxious, unsure, unmotivated... welcome! You are NOT alone! And those feelings are not your destiny, and they don't have to be your driver. You can choose right now to do what is in your heart anyway!

<u>What has God put in your heart? What is one way you can serve today?</u>

<u>What is the place of obedience He has called you to?</u>

Today is the day to take action and allow your feelings to catch up!

"And without faith living within us it would be impossible to please God. For we come to God in faith knowing that he is real and that he rewards the faith of those who passionately seek him."
Hebrews 11:6 TPT

Have you ever found yourself out of rhythm?

It took me years to create a morning routine. It has been messy, imperfect, unstructured, and inconsistent. But I never stopped trying.

Finally, I found my groove. Recently though, I've been prompted to disrupt the pattern. I never want my time with the Lord to become stale and insignificant. I don't want to treat my time with him as a task completed.

When this happens the routine may be present but you are out of rhythm.

Not long ago my husband and I were in church with some dear friends in Texas. During his powerful sermon, he quoted the verse below. Amidst so many passages shared, it was this verse that anchored in my heart and didn't let go. I love those moments. The next morning, I changed the routine. I leaned into this verse and all that it means. I used my voice to speak to my father. I laid out the pieces of my life before him.

Day 19

The pieces that are broken and the ones that are whole. Because sometimes the broken is ready to be healed. And sometimes, the whole things are ready to be broken. I laid out the overwhelming and I laid out the insignificant.

Because sometimes the overwhelming aren't important after all. And sometimes the insignificant are the greatest above all.

Then I waited. I waited with expectation. I waited in worship. I waited for His fire to fall upon my heart. Because without it, nothing else matters.

Perhaps you've been in routine but out of rhythm. Perhaps you've yet to make the time to spend. Can I encourage you? It may be messy, but lay it out anyway, because it MATTERS.

"At each and every sunrise you will hear my voice as I prepare my sacrifice of prayer to you. Every morning I lay out the pieces of my life on the altar and wait for your fire to fall upon my heart."
Psalms 5:3 TPT

How do I eliminate shame of the past and anxiety of the future?

You can't steward your past or your future because neither is in your possession.

You can only steward the present.

You can learn from the past, draw from your experiences, and appreciate what was. I encourage all of those things. But you cannot steward a thing that is already gone.

You can plan and prepare for your future. Dream for what is possible. Expect more and imagine your desired outcome and future self. I encourage all of those things! But you cannot steward today what isn't promised in tomorrow.

The only thing you can steward is the present. What do I have today? The relationships, the people I interact with, the time in my day, the finances in my hands, the gifts and talents I currently possess, and the knowledge I hold. These are the things I currently have.

Plan for your future but plow in the now. A very wise man said these words to me recently, "We plan in years but we live in moments."

What moment are you in right now?

Can you appreciate the magic in it? Can you learn from the adversity?

Can you make this one count as if it were your last?

Can you steward it to become the seed of tomorrow's harvest?

"But seek first his kingdom and his righteousness, and all these things will be given to you as well. Therefore do not worry about tomorrow, for tomorrow will worry about itself. Each day has enough trouble of its own."
Matthew 6:33-34 NIV

What if we're completely off in how we see the mountain we're up against?

I've been there, facing what feels like an enormous, unmovable mountain in front of me. You know, one of those situations that just seem way too big to conquer? I get it, trust me.

In those times, it's like the circumstances are looming over you, threatening to engulf you. But here's the kicker:

What if, when we're standing face to face with our mountain, we choose to believe that the very same God who took us to its peak can also make it crumble before us?

After all, He's gifted us with this faith that can move mountains.
But here's a thought: What if that mountain isn't out to wreck us, divert us, or mess us up? What if, beyond its daunting presence, it's got a mission way grander than itself?

You know, when something small shifts, it often goes unnoticed. But when a mountain budges, everyone stops and takes notice! We're not at the mercy of mountains— they're the ones at our mercy! And here's the thing, what message are we sending out there about our God through all this? What if our mountain-moving faith could actually show the world just how incredible our God is?

Perhaps we need to adjust how we're seeing these mountains.

Maybe, just maybe, they're opportunities for us to showcase our faith, our courage, and the awe-inspiring power of our God. After all, moving mountains is our thing! And when we move them, we're not just changing our own story; we're giving the world a glimpse of the incredible things God can do.

Listen to the truth I speak to you: If someone says to this mountain with great faith and having no doubt, 'Mountain, be lifted up and thrown into the midst of the sea,' and believes that what he says will happen, it will be done.
Mark 11:23 TPT

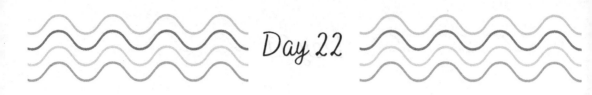

It's Time to Clap Louder!!

Do you know what that does? It drowns out those nagging insecurities that sometimes creep in. And let me tell you, as I'm journeying through life; I'm realizing the immense value of surrounding myself with women who genuinely cheer for other women.

Here's the scoop: every single one of us is a force to be reckoned with. We've got strength flowing through our veins, we're packing serious power, we're each uniquely crafted with the utmost care, and we're equipped with talents that are nothing short of strategic brilliance. And the cherry on top?

The One who designed us loves us unconditionally and embraces us just as we are, flaws and all. What if we not only believed this about ourselves but also held it true for our sisters?

Let's get real here—dimming someone else's light won't make yours shine any brighter. All it does is let more darkness seep in.

So, let's flip the script. This week, let's make a conscious effort to raise the roof for others. Because here's the twist: when someone else is rocking it in one area, it doesn't take away from your shine. Actually, it's quite the opposite! When the tide rises, all the ships rise along with it.

So, let's surround ourselves with those who are on the upswing, even if their path looks different from ours.

Here's to crafting a culture where applause and celebration are the name of the game! And a heartfelt shoutout to all of the amazing women who make this look easy. You all make me a better version of myself, and for that, I'm incredibly grateful!

"Let your light so shine before men, that they may see your good works,
and glorify your Father which is in heaven. In the same way, let your light shine before others, so that they may see your good works and give glory to your Father who is in heaven."
Matthew 5:16 NIV

Ever pondered the company you keep?

Those individuals who infuse your life with positivity and make you believe you could conquer anything, just like God by your side?

Well, my friend, I'm here to tell you that you're granted the divine nod to spend more time with that uplifting crew.

Now, let's delve deeper into the ones who drain your energy and dim your light. They might not align with your true circle, but guess what? Loving them doesn't mean you're tethered to their negativity. It's about recognizing that God has called you to a life of freedom, and that includes shaking off those energy-sappers.

In the grand script of life, you're not a passive character; you're the author of your atmosphere.

Instead of merely reflecting the energy around you, picture yourself as a thermostat, setting the tone.

So, take this as your divine directive to seek your tribe of positivity and step away from the comfortable but confining spaces.

From a biblical standpoint, I can testify to the incredible circle God has orchestrated around me. It's a reminder of how He longs to bless us beyond our imagination. Remember, the Bible speaks of iron sharpening iron—surrounding ourselves with positive influences helps us grow in faith. So, let's journey forward, guided by faith and empowered by uplifting connections.

"Walk with the wise and become wise; associate with fools and get in trouble." Proverbs 13:20 NLT

Ever struggle with your identity and worth?

I recently stumbled upon a scripture that practically leaped off the page and into my heart! It's Hebrews 11:24 from TPT. *"Faith enabled Moses to choose God's will, for although he was raised as the son of Pharaoh's daughter, he refused to make that his identity."*

Moses flat-out rejected the idea of being defined by his upbringing. He refused to allow his past to define his future. How many of us have let our past, our mistakes, or even our family background define us, holding us in chains?

But guess what? You don't have to stay in that place! You're the captain of your identity ship. When I embraced Jesus, I also embraced His identity for me. When I feel enslaved to negative thoughts or words I ask myelf one powerful question. **"SAYS WHO?"** Whose idea was that? Who spoke that to you or over you? Whose voice are you listening to?

If it didn't originate in heaven, it shouldn't dominate on earth!

After every negative thought or comment, challenge it with that phrase. You get to decide whose words shape your identity. My prayer as a mama is that my husband and I would have the loudest voice in our kids' lives as they grow to speak life over them and shape them into their God given identity.

Should we not also desire to be the loudest voice in our own lives as we echo our Heavenly Father's voice and declare His words?

Guess what? You can do this too! If Moses could break free from his circumstances and refuse to let them define him, so can we. It's all about believing in the identity that God has planned for us. Let's break those chains, embrace our true identity, and rise to our full potential!

"I knew you before I formed you in your mother's womb. Before you were born I set you apart and appointed you as my prophet to the nations."
Jeremiah 1:5 NLT

"The secret of change is to focus all of your energy not o fighting the old but on building the new." Socrates

Sometimes we pour our energy, time, and even prayers into battling the old stuff. But what if we flipped the script a bit? What if we poured that same energy into chasing after our goals and dreams?

Imagine if we shifted our focus from what we need to let go of, to what we need to embrace and grow in! Instead of struggling to stop one thing, how about replacing it with starting something productive and fruitful?

The Bible says, "Magnify the Lord." What we fix our gaze upon becomes bigger in our view.

Yet we often end up magnifying the negative. Gratefully, the Bible guides us on what to think about, meditate on, and fill our minds with. Now, here's the real deal—it's one thing to know it and a whole other ball game to put it into practice.

Here's how it looks in real life:
Swap those complaints for gratitude.
Replace negative "what ifs" with positive ones.
When frustration knocks, answer with a big dose of intentional joy.

When something's sucking the life out of you, unplug and seek what brings you back to life and joy. Ditch the TV, radio, and social media, and tune into sermons, podcasts, or audiobooks that flood your heart and mind with life-giving words. You don't have to tackle a mountain of tasks today—start with just one! Be aware and intentional. Your growth? Well, that's in your hands. You're not stuck in a repeating cycle—you have the power to change it.

Just remember, if nothing changes, then, well, nothing changes!

"Finally, brothers and sisters, whatever is true, whatever is noble, whatever is right, whatever is pure, whatever is lovely, whatever is admirable—if anything is excellent or praiseworthy—think about such things."
Philippians 4:8 NIV

Day 26

ANTS & a Positive Mindset!!

Ever dealt with those pesky ants? Well, I'm not talking insects here—I mean our Automatic Negative Thought System. They're like an army, showing up uninvited.

Our brains have a knack for negativity—it's a survival mechanism. But guess what? We're not running from danger these days. So why are our stress signals still on high alert?

Time to take charge! Recognize these thoughts and turn the tables. The Bible's got our back too—it tells us to grab every thought and focus on what's good.

When a thought knocks, question it:

- Is this even true?
- Is it 100% true? (Perfect for those pesky "always" and "never" thoughts.)
- Is this thought doing any good for me or others?
- What if the exact opposite were true? What then?
- Can I find a reason to be thankful here?

Gratitude shifts perspectives and opens up joy. And you know what's awesome? Goodness is everywhere!

Chase goodness and you'll find it. But here's the real secret:

Seek God first.

He's the peace-maker, joy-bringer, strength-provider, mind-transformer, and life-giver.

The Bible says when you diligently seek Him you will find Him. And with Him comes every good gift. He is a good Father.

"Do not conform to the pattern of this world, but be transformed by the renewing of your mind. Then you will be able to test and approve what God's will is—his good, pleasing and perfect will."
Romans 12:2 NIV

Looking ahead with purpose!

Have you ever stood on the shoreline and looked out over the cascading ocean waters as waves continually crashed in? There is so much possibility on the horizon but you are stuck standing on the shoreline of promise simply waiting and ready to accept only what washes in over your feet on the shoreline.

Here's a thought to mull over: Are you content with waiting for the future, or are you forging it with today's actions and routines?

Let's keep it real—I used to play the waiting game, hoping destiny would roll in. But these past years, life's teachings have hit home. Nowadays, I'm all about strategic steps and heartfelt prayers for what lies ahead.

I'm embracing the call to step onto uncertain waters, venturing into the unfamiliar, and taking strides beyond my comfort zone.

It's about diving into the unconventional, even if it's a bit misunderstood. Trust me, there's something stirring inside.

I'm diving deep into the dreams God's etched into my heart. Today's tasks are tomorrow's building blocks, and I'm leaning into them.

So, I'm curious, is this resonating with you? That inner tug, that sense of something remarkable brewing this season? It's not fading for me, and I'm wondering if you're feeling it too.

Take a moment and pen the things stirring in your heart! And pay attention, friend, those are often the whispers of a divine calling.

"Commit to the Lord whatever you do,
and he will establish your plans."
Proverbs 16:3 NIV

"Wouldn't that be something!" OR "Possibility awaits!"

<u>Ever stop and think about what leaps to mind when you see someone living a life that looks different from yours?</u>

We've been here, there, and everywhere lately. From breathtaking retreats to sunny getaways... It's been a whirlwind, honestly. Ministry & memories and everything in between. I used to watch folks living out a life I secretly craved and thought, "Wow, wouldn't that be something!"

Here's the revelation: envy and comparison only rear their heads for things you genuinely yearn for. You can genuinely cheer on someone's success while also aspiring to it yourself. That's where my journey took a turn—from "wouldn't that be something" to "why not me?"

I'm convinced God doesn't reveal more to taunt us; it's a divine invite to step into greater things. But here's the catch: you have to believe you're capable and deserving. You have to know that if they can, you can too!

I got fed up with seeing others leading healthy lives and thinking, "Wouldn't that be something." Tired of witnessing folks enjoying flexibility and meaningful travel, blessing their families, and thinking, "Wouldn't that be something." I was over seeing people impact the world with passion, purpose, and joy, and believing it was only possible for them.

No more—I decided, "Why not me?" So I got up and took that initial step. I shifted my mindset and got curious. What's their secret sauce? How do they think? What daily habits are they rocking? What are their beliefs and disciplines?

Because if "they" can, trust me, you can too! The next time you catch yourself thinking, "Wouldn't that be something," I challenge you to pause and ponder: "Why not me?"

"I can do all things through Christ who strengthens me."
Philippians 4:13 NKJV

You know, it's funny—my natural tendency, or let's say MY natural tendency, is to wait until the whole staircase is crystal clear before I take that first step. Alright, I might be selling myself a bit short—I'd settle for at least half the staircase in view.

But then I wonder, where's the faith in that? This season of my life, I'm flipping the script. I'm choosing to lean into the things that scare me, rather than giving them the cold shoulder.

The most obedient steps often come to us one at a time.

They come with their fair share of fear, pain, doubt, and yes, a bit of trembling. Tears and uncertainty? You bet. In fact, I'm learning they're the very bricks these steps are made of.

Actually, that's where the magic happens—these obedience steps are also rooted in faith. Faith in God's promises. Faith that delights Him. It's the kind of faith that's not about our skills or comprehension but about syncing up with Him,

His plans, His agenda. Without understanding the entire process, with only a glimpse of what could be... guess what? Start anyway! Right where you are, with whatever you've got. Because here's the kicker:

He's more than enough. He's enough to bridge the gaps, outdo expectations, and carry us further than our wildest dreams.

I'm not at the finish line waving back at you. Nope, I'm right on that first step, moving forward alongside you. Yeah, I might be shaking a bit, but I'm taking that step. We can both lock our eyes on God's promises and celebrate His faithfulness with each and every step. Let's do this together!

"Never doubt God's mighty power to work in you and accomplish all this. He will achieve infinitely more than your greatest request, your most unbelievable dream, and exceed your wildest imagination! He will outdo them all, for his miraculous power constantly energizes you."
Ephesians 3:20 TPT

Let's take a moment to step back from the rush and really absorb the present.

Pause for a breath, and let me ask you this:
What fills your heart with genuine gratitude today?

In the hustle and bustle, it's easy to get swept up in putting out fires and addressing one issue after another. We strive for progress, for betterment, but do we truly pause to soak in and appreciate what's already present?

Today, I find gratitude in:
The quiet, unhurried morning that allowed my family and me to gather around the kitchen table to share laughter, stories, and the simple pleasure of good coffee.

The helping hands that showed up at church today, stepping in with generosity and support. The unwavering love of my incredible husband—a constant reminder of the depth of affection. The sound of my children's laughter echoing through the house, a sweet symphony of joy.

Day 30

The anticipation of an upcoming journey with our company and close friends. A time of learning, growth, and bonding. The profound worship experience during yesterday's service, beautifully led by our devoted team. The impactful sermon delivered by my husband, which truly resonated with me.

Now, let's be real—life doesn't always present itself perfectly. It's interspersed with disappointments and unavoidable distractions.
But here's the gem of wisdom:

Choose gratitude, deliberately and consistently.

In the midst of life's imperfections, let's train ourselves to notice the intricate beauty. Let's actively cultivate thankfulness for the blessings that envelop us. Each day is an opportunity to wear the lens of gratitude to experience the richness of life in its entirety.

"Give thanks in all circumstances;
for this is God's will for you in Christ Jesus."
1 Thessalonians 5:18 NIV

How do we partner well in marriage and life?

Together, we navigate the twists and turns, embracing all facets of life—parenting, ministry, business, joys, trials, and more.

Someone asked me recently how my spouse and I keep our marriage a priority amid the chaos. While there's no one-size-fits-all answer, here are the key points that resonate with me:

1. **Commitment** It's more than just a promise; it's a steadfast choice to weather all storms together. We opt for happiness over misery, even when it's harder. It's about unwavering dedication and walking this path as a united front.

2. **Communication** This requires intentional effort and vulnerability. We seek understanding over being understood, prioritizing resolution over being right. Seeking outside guidance when needed has enriched this journey.

3. **Clarity** Keep your goals and aspirations crystal clear. Understand what you both want and why. Continuously define your shared vision to stay aligned.

4. **Creativity** After two decades of marriage, we've learned to infuse creativity. Regularly date your spouse, break routines, and inject spontaneity. Embrace the new to keep the spark alive.

5. **Center on Christ** Our faith is the foundation. Individually pursuing Christ aligns us as a couple. This shared commitment makes Christ the core of our marriage and home.

In the end, it's about choosing unity, communication, clarity, creativity, and Christ as the center.

"Two are better than one, because they have a good return for their labor: If either of them falls down, one can help the other up."
Ecclesiastes 4:9-10a NIV

Feeling a little stirred up or maybe even downright uncomfortable?

Let me share an intriguing eagle story that speaks volumes. See, eagles are known for their majestic nests, but do you know what goes into creating them? The mother eagle starts by layering the nest with thorns, rocks, and sharp materials that seem out of place for a place of rest. Yet, after the foundation is laid, she lines it with a cozy padding of feathers, fur, and softer materials. This is where she lays her eggs and nurtures her chicks.

Now, here's the twist: when those chicks grow into fledglings, something interesting unfolds.

The mother eagle deliberately starts "stirring up the nest."

With her talons, she brings the thorns and rocks back to the surface, displacing the comfortable padding. Why? To prompt her young ones to leave the familiar nest and take flight.

If you're feeling stirred and a tad uncomfortable, take it as a positive sign! If the nest remained overly cozy, you'd never feel the urge to soar. Remember, your destiny isn't confined to your comfort zone; it's about reaching new heights.

So, spread your wings and take that leap of faith! Trust in the Creator who fashioned you, nurtured you, and yes, stirred up your circumstances to push you out of your comfort zone. He lovingly rearranges your "home" to breed enough discomfort and frustration that will cause you step out. Perhaps your next nest is waiting for you to build it!

You're equipped for this new journey, and incredible heights await your ascent!

"but those who hope in the Lord will renew their strength. They will soar on wings like eagles; they will run and not grow weary, they will walk and not be faint."
Isaiah 40:31 NIV

Have you ever felt unsure and unqualified?

I spent so many years of my life lacking confidence and self-worth. I felt like I was too much for some people and not enough for others.

I was exhausted trying to conform to an image I wasn't created for.

Gratefully, God gifted me with a husband who spent years telling me all that he saw inside of me. He had enough belief in me to borrow until I could find my own. Who could you be that gift for?

It took work. It took not quitting when everything in me wanted to throw in the towel. It took leaning in when it got uncomfortable and facing fear head on without bowing to it. It continues to take the inner work that isn't seen and it sure isn't pretty. But it's worth it. Here are my top tips today.

1. Surround yourself with people that believe bigger for you and won't allow you to settle for less.

2. When it gets hard, dig in. Failure isn't final, so embrace it as your teacher.

3. The inner work is messy. But you can't bypass it. Your self-worth and confidence are your responsibility.

4. When you chase something greater than yourself, you should feel afraid. Small dreams are like small prayers; they insult the greatness inside you and the greatness of the one who created you!

5. If your circle doesn't celebrate when you finally stand on your stage, find a new circle.

6. When people in your life stand on their stage, clap the loudest for them even if they arrive before you! If we can't celebrate others, we aren't ready for ours.

7. Learning to believe bigger isn't selfish! You'll need enough belief for the people in your life to borrow until they find their own.

Now go on: Do it so big that only heaven can get the credit!!

"Put your heart and soul into every activity you do, as though you are doing it for the Lord himself and not merely for others."
Colossians 3:23 TPT

Have you ever learned from the most unexpected teacher?

During a church service not long ago, my eyes landed on something truly remarkable. A few rows back, there she stood, this little girl perched on her grandparents' chair, fully immersed in worship. Her fervor was a sight to behold.

What struck me even more was that it felt like looking in a mirror. Her keen eyes were locked onto me, tracking my every move. When I lifted my hand, she mirrored the gesture. If I directed my gaze upwards, so did she. When my hand covered my heart, and my head bowed in reverence, she echoed the same. Even my swaying motion was replicated by her.

Not a soul in that congregation worshipped with the same intensity as she did. It got me thinking - **when did we lose that unshakable faith?** What if we reclaimed just a fraction of her childlike belief, enough to emulate the actions of another person, believing that we too could partake in what they're experiencing?

Perhaps she isn't fully aware of the profoundness of what she's doing. But what if, in her innocent eyes, she saw me encountering something divine? What if, without hesitation, she joined in, fully expecting to encounter the same? Unburdened by others' opinions, untouched by doubts of unworthiness or qualification, she exhibited pure surrender and abandon.

Oh, to regain the heart of a child in the presence of our Father.

I can't help but wonder: what if we all embraced this sweet girl's unreserved heart? What if we dared to believe that we could share in the same divine experiences? What if we laid down our pride and preoccupations long enough to truly encounter God?

"And he said: 'Truly I tell you, unless you change and become like little children, you will never enter the kingdom of heaven.'"
Matthew 18:3 NIV

How have you transformed in the last 5 years?

I certainly hope the answer is yes! There's no time to waste.

Can you look back with gratitude and appreciation for your own growth and journey to become?

When you take the time to appreciate the journey, you can value the process even more than the result. Here is my story of "Becoming Her."

Becoming her took courage that I didn't know I had. Becoming her took burying pain that I didn't mean to carry. Becoming her meant asking for help when I didn't know the next step. Becoming her took admitting that I couldn't do it alone. Becoming her meant being vulnerable when I felt afraid. Becoming her took faith when I had no other choice.

Becoming her meant I had to learn what I wished I had already known. Becoming her meant leaning in when I wanted to run away. Becoming her meant getting up every time I would fall, even if I was falling over the same obstacle as before. Becoming her meant refusing to quit when I didn't think I had it in me. Becoming her meant refusing to settle when good felt good enough.

Becoming her meant not caring what others thought, even when their voices often confirmed my own fears and insecurities. Becoming her meant becoming a student of my mistakes instead of a slave to them. Becoming her meant using prayer as a weapon for war rather than a hall pass to avoid the battle.

Becoming her meant saying no to good things to be able to say yes to greater ones. Becoming her wasn't easy... but I'm standing here thanking the me of yesterday. Before she knew what the journey would hold, she said yes to taking the first step. With as much gratitude as you have for yourself as you look back, may there be even more expectation as you look ahead.

You aren't finished yet!! Who will you decide to become?

"Do not conform to the pattern of this world, but be transformed by the renewing of your mind."
Romans 12:2 NIV

How do words shape our reality?

In the journey of life, we often overlook the incredible influence of the words we speak – especially the words we speak to ourselves. The older I get the more I have come to understand the weight our words carry.

Raising two teenagers has heightened my awareness of this truth. I listen carefully to the words they speak because I understand they are shaping their beliefs, identity, and futures.

I am always reminded that words are more than mere utterances; they're powerful agents of creation, like a currency that determines the trajectory of our lives.

However, it's not just *their* words that I pay attention to. I must also take inventory of *my own* words and the thoughts that give rise to them. It's a gradual process, a journey of rewriting the narratives we've embraced. It calls for intentional choices in what we meditate on and how we speak – not just about ourselves, but about others as well.

Proverbs 18:21 reminds us that the power of life and death resides in our tongues. This truth is profound, challenging us to grasp the significance of our spoken and thought words. I firmly believe that if we cease to echo our current circumstances, we'll begin to witness a transformation – as we dare to vocalize the realities we're believing, hoping, and striving for. As you embark on this day, let's reflect on the statement that resonates within you.

Are your words breathing life into your dreams and aspirations or inadvertently limiting them?

Let's harness the incredible power of words to align our inner dialogues with the abundant life God desires for us. After all, our words are not just words – they're vehicles that carry us toward the future we envision.

"The tongue has the power of life and death,
and those who love it will eat its fruit."
Proverbs 18:21 NIV

Does "new" feel uncertain and unsettling?

Change often comes with discomfort, uncertainty, and the challenge of forging new paths. A couple of years ago, our family experienced one of those significant shifts – what we fondly refer to as a "divine interruption." We left the comfort of a city we called home, responding to a higher calling that beckoned us toward a new season and purpose.

Amidst these transitions in life, I've realized that isolation can be a formidable adversary, especially for women.

We may struggle to prioritize ourselves and build close-knit friendships. I've faced this battle and discovered that while it might demand effort, intention, and vulnerability, cultivating authentic relationships is worth every ounce of discomfort. Although I'm already blessed with a tribe of incredible relationships, the call to create community in our new surroundings tugged at my heart. So, I took deliberate steps toward it.

Let me share a lesson learned: When you're lacking something, shift from complaining to creating. I've dabbled in both, and without a doubt, the act of creating has yielded more fruitful results.

As I have taken steps, the walls of reservation begin slowly coming down, paving the way for new individuals to experience the love of God through human relationships.

Consider this: What if today, you took that leap – made that phone call or extended that coffee invitation?

Imagine the potential for powerful, life-giving communities that could emerge from those small steps. Embracing newness might be uncomfortable, but within that discomfort lies the opportunity to craft connections that enrich our lives and echo God's design for community.

"As iron sharpens iron, so one person sharpens another."
Proverbs 27:17 NIV

Day 38

Do you ever fall into the trap of comparison?

I understand the allure and the pitfalls of the social media era we live in. It's so easy to scroll through carefully curated feeds and wonder why our own lives don't seem to measure up. Comparison becomes the thief of our joy, and we find ourselves stuck in a cycle of exhaustion and discontentment. But let me remind you today there's a reality beyond the filters and poses.

Why do we waste our precious energy comparing our journey to others'?

Our uniqueness gets drowned out by the noise of comparison, robbing us of the joy that should accompany our journey. Often, what we see in others' profiles is a polished version, while we're in the midst of our unfiltered, unedited reality.

Here's the truth: You're not behind, late, unlucky, or unworthy. You're on a journey – a journey that's uniquely yours. The only way you fall behind is if you stop running your race, comparing it to someone else's. You weren't created for someone else's path; you were designed for your own.

Let's debunk the myth that the grass is greener on the other side. In reality, it's greener where you water it.

Remember, when you see someone else's supposedly perfect life online, you're often glimpsing at their highlights reel, not the full picture. It's like admiring a perfectly manicured lawn, not realizing it's astroturf rolled out for a photo shoot.

So keep going, my friend. Embrace your journey and savor every moment. Laugh in the midst of challenges. Bask in the warmth of life's sunshine. Aspire to more, dream bigger, and stretch beyond your comfort zone.

And above all, keep running your race at your pace.

"Each one should test their own actions. Then they can take pride in themselves alone, without comparing themselves to someone else, for each one should carry their own load."
Galatians 6:4-5 NIV

How much power do your words really hold?

James 3:4-5 paints a powerful image, comparing ships to our tongues. Ships, though massive and driven by fierce winds, are controlled by a tiny rudder directed by the one at the helm. Similarly, our tongues may seem small, yet they wield tremendous influence. Just as a small spark can ignite a vast forest, our words can have a monumental impact on our own lives and the lives of those around us.

Just imagine how a slight adjustment in our words could alter the trajectory of our lives.

Here are practical steps to apply this wisdom:

1. **Awareness** Reflect on your daily words. Are they positive, faith-filled, and uplifting? Recognizing your speech patterns is the first step toward transformation.
2. **Affirmations** Incorporate daily affirmations. As you juggle multiple roles, these declarations of faith can ground you in God's truth.

3. **Pause** Before speaking, pause and consider your words' impact. Choose words aligned with your values and God's principles.
4. **Encouragement** Use words to uplift others. A simple compliment can brighten someone's day.
5. **Prayerful Communication** Seek wisdom in your conversations. Let the Holy Spirit guide your speech.
6. **Reflection** Review your interactions. Make adjustments to ensure your words align with God's truth.

Let's remember that our words have transformative power.

"Do not let any unwholesome talk come out of your mouths, but only what is helpful for building others up according to their needs, that it may benefit those who listen."
Ephesians 4:29 NIV

Do you ever feel like shrinking vs. shining?

It's easy to feel like we should downplay our strengths and accomplishments, especially as women. But guess what? That's not what God wants for us.

God wants you to shine without hesitation. He wants you to embrace who you are in Him and boldly showcase the incredible gifts and talents He's given you.

So, here's a little reminder for you today: Don't dim your light. Don't shrink back. Don't apologize for being amazing, for being unique, for being exactly who you are.

Your life, with all its twists and turns, successes and struggles, is a masterpiece in progress. And guess what? God wants that masterpiece to be seen.

Remember, you were never meant to play small.

Day 40

You were created to shine brilliantly. Embrace your voice, find your strength, and step into courage.

You are an embodiment of God's glory, and that's something to be celebrated, not hidden.

So, go ahead, shine your light. Let it illuminate every corner of your life. And don't you dare apologize for it. You are fearfully and wonderfully made, and every part of you has a purpose in God's grand plan.

May your light shine brighter than ever before, touching the lives of those around you.

"Don't hide your light! Let it shine for all; let your good deeds glow for all to see, so that they will praise your heavenly Father."
Matthew 5:15-16 TLB

Do you need to be ignited and activated today?

"She woke up this day with passion in her heart and fire in her bones, and she refused to settle! She committed to never again shrink to someone else's standards and determined within herself to shed every weight so she could soar as she was always intended to! This is her day to live as her creator designed her, without bowing to the imposed limitations of other created things. And without hesitation, she invited others to shake off their own shackles, rise up, and soar!"
Heather Ann Wallace

Have you ever woken up with a burning desire to break free from the chains that hold you back? That's the fire of purpose within you, urging you to rise above and embrace your true potential.

The journey towards becoming who you were meant to be starts with a bold decision.

It's about waking up with passion, refusing to settle, and shedding the weight hindering your flight. We live in a world that often tries to confine us to its standards and limitations.

But as children of God, we were created to soar beyond those boundaries.

When we place our hope and trust in the Lord, we tap into a wellspring of strength and courage.

Like eagles, we can soar above challenges and limitations. So, today, commit to living as the person God designed you to be. Embrace your uniqueness, discard the weights that hold you down, and invite others to join you on this journey of freedom and purpose.

Imagine the impact we could make if we all rose up and embraced our true selves. Let's be the inspiration that encourages others to break free and soar alongside us. Remember, you were created to rise, to shine, and to make a difference in this world.

"Let me be clear, the Anointed One has set us free—not partially, but completely and wonderfully free! We must always cherish this truth and stubbornly refuse to go back into the bondage of our past."
Galatians 5:1 TPT

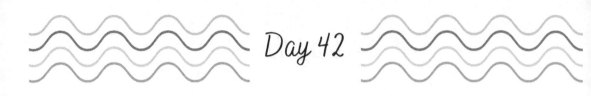

What is the difference between overcome and override?

This often gets misconstrued: the difference between overriding and overcoming. In this journey we call life, seeking help isn't a sign of weakness; in fact, it's a remarkable demonstration of strength and courage. The trap is to believe that your life, your decisions, your circumstances are soley impacting and affecting you. But I have come to learn that it's not just about us—

It's about those who will benefit from the battles we've conquered.

Remember the story of Samson in the Bible? He found honey in the carcass of a lion, feeding not just himself but his family, too. Sometimes, the compassion we show ourselves through seeking help prepares us for the people we'll cross paths with in the future. These experiences are meant to equip us for divine connections ahead.

So, let's shift our perspective. This moment isn't about creating a monument to our struggles; it's about embracing a temporary season that will eventually lead to greater victory.

It's about arming ourselves with the wisdom and strength we'll use to uplift and support those who need it down the road.

Let's recognize that our growth is a gift not just to us, but to a world waiting to be impacted by our strength and resilience.

What you kill today may very well provide the nourishment you and others need for tomorrow!

"He gives strength to the weary and increases the power of the weak."
Isaiah 40:29 NIV

Do you ever struggle with impatience?

I have been so impatient. I want so badly to add "in times past" to that statement, but the truth is I have been so impatient today, yesterday, and the day before. I have been like Sarah in the Bible when God promised to give her children in her old age. She believed in the promise but wanted to help God along in fulfilling it. Since we are all being honest here, I bet you have, too!

When God speaks, I listen! His word is provident. It is sure. It is steady. It does not fail. And it does not delay! But so often, I have perceived just that....delay. I have set God on my terms and timetable rather than submitting to and trusting His.

I can look back and see when I have given up, thrown in the towel, or walked away too soon. It didn't happen when I thought it should. It didn't happen as quickly as it did for them. The path to the promise was difficult. The goal and dream ahead weren't as visible as the rocks in the road I find myself stumbling over on the path to get there.

Some promises manifest instantly. But all promises manifest!

Did you read that? Go back and read it again.

All. Promises. Manifest.

Usually, the process to the promise is meant to enlarge YOUR capacity to be able to contain and steward what God has destined for you. If He spoke it- He will fulfill it.

So pursue that dream! Take that step of faith! Build that business! Start that foundation! Preach that message! Create that new thing. If God has whispered it in your heart.... Trust His word to put it in your Hand!

Slowly. Steadily. Surely. The vision will be fulfilled.

"But these things I plan won't happen right away. Slowly, steadily, surely, the time approaches when the vision will be fulfilled. If it seems slow, be patient! For it will surely take place. It will not be late by a single day."
Habakkuk 2:3 TLB

How to navigate uncertainty?

Do you remember the year 2020? Wow! What a doozy that was. And what an incredible teacher for turbulent times we will undoubtedly encounter again

We have all encountered a realm of unfamiliarity, stirring up feelings of fear, anxiety, frustration, anger, and grief. It's easy to let these emotions take center stage. But what if we reframed this chapter of our lives? What if we chose to see it as a divine interruption?

What if, amid the uncertainty, we shifted our perspective from despair to expectation?

Admittedly, this mindset shift requires effort – a conscious decision to replace worry with hope. In these moments when the path ahead seems foggy, we have an anchor. We can lean into the One who guides us through the unknown. So, take a deep breath, my friend, and rename this chapter of your journey.

Remember, it's not over yet, and every twist and turn is still orchestrated for our good and His glory!

Redirect your gaze! Adjust your focus! Instead of retreating or holding back, let's step forward and grow. Cultivating expectation becomes the fertile soil where miracles bloom. Miracles in our families, in our finances, in our health, in our ministries, in our businesses, and right in the heart of our homes.

Let's embrace this divine interruption with faith. Let's open our hearts to the unexpected, knowing that the Author of our story is orchestrating something beautiful amid the chaos. Keep expecting, keep hoping, and watch as the miraculous unfold in every corner of your life!

"Forget the former things; do not dwell on the past. See, I am doing a new thing! Now it springs up; do you not perceive it? I am making a way in the wilderness and streams in the wasteland."
Isaiah 43:18-19 NIV

How do you stand on the battle ground?

The battle is hard. The resistance rises. The storms surge. The obstacles surmount. The opposition grows. The waves crash one after another and we feel as though we can barely catch our next breath. But what if we embraced the inevitable and shifted our perspective?

The battle you're facing today will be the bridge used to cross into your destiny. It isn't in the way of your path; it IS your path!

Overcoming that obstacle is what opens the door for what's next. The strength you gain, the confidence that grows, the mindset you obtain all comes from within the battle itself.

In Joshua 6, the Israelites were pursuing a promise held within fortified walls. It seemed impossible. They didn't have the tools necessary to overtake the obstacle. But they had a promise. So they walked... in circles. How frustrating must it have been to circle their promise repeatedly and not make any visible progress?

But actually, progress was made! It was the progress of obedience.

It was the progress of taking the steps even when they didn't see the result. It was the resilience of the journey and the refusal to quit.

They pursued, and they persevered! And they didn't just stop with the action; they shifted the posture of their heart. It wasn't enough to take the steps; they had to overcome their own thoughts and begin to praise and shout for the victory they had not yet seen. That's the preface we often overlook when walls "suddenly" come crashing down.

Make no mistake, the "suddenly" is always preceded by a process. But when the battle was won, the very walls that once walled them out from the promise are believed to have become the ramps that carried them in. The battle is necessary and the victory is promised. So take heart, friends!! What you're facing isn't blocking you, it is making you! And the very thing facing you will bow and become the ramp into your destiny.

"But thanks be to God! He gives us the victory through our Lord Jesus Christ."
1 Corinthians 15:57 NIV

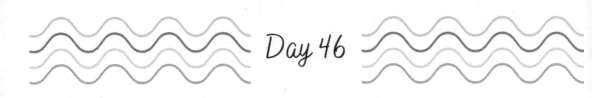

Hi, I'm Heather and I'm a recovering control freak and avid planner.

I am still on the journey of learning the power of surrendering control. You see, I used to be the ultimate planner, the queen of wanting to know every detail. Sound familiar?

But here's the twist: God has a sense of humor. I can almost picture Him chuckling when I try to map out my life down to the tiniest detail. Not out of mockery, but in the loving way a parent looks at their child trying to grasp the concept of a long road trip and the incessant question, "Are we there yet?" It's like He's saying, "Ah, there's my daughter, weaving her plans while I've got something extraordinary in store."

And here's the beautiful part. Remember those road trips with little ones? They couldn't quite comprehend the journey or its purpose; they had to simply trust that we were leading them to an incredible destination. In much the same way, God gazes upon us with love as we strive to chart our course.

He delights in our efforts and appreciates our questions, but in the grand scheme, He reassures us that the journey—with all its twists, turns, questions, and detours—is worth the wait.

Please understand I'm not suggesting we toss planning out the window. Rather, I'm inviting you to embrace a flexible mindset. Our plans may pivot unexpectedly, but we can trust the ultimate Navigator who reroutes us toward His purpose. His guidance will never steer us wrong. His destination is worth the journey, my friend. It's worth the uncertainty and the surprises, the roadblocks and the winding roads.

So as you journey forward, remember that the detours don't define you. They refine you. The unexpected turns are opportunities for God's ultimate purpose to prevail. And trust me, it will be more spectacular than you could ever plan.

"Many are the plans in a person's heart, but it is the Lord's purpose that prevails."
Proverbs 19:21 NIV

I used to say, "I don't need to be on the stage."

Hear me out before you shut me down. Before I became a pastor myself, I was "the pastor's wife." For so long, I believed that in order to fulfill that beautiful role, I must not only serve in the background but also enjoy it there. It wasn't until later in life that I discovered that fulfilling my calling didn't mean forsaking my husband's. I can be a pastor's wife and serve in that capacity while also operating in my own unique gifts as well.

So although I don't *need* a literal stage, I very much need a platform. I need a space to pour out. That space has taken on many forms and shapes over the years.

Sometimes it was the heart of grieving mother; other times it was the ear of broken-hearted teenager. Many times it has been the heart of my home speaking into my husband and children. It has been a microphone speaking into audience of thousands and it has been an iPhone screen on social media. But at my core, I was created for it.

I needed to stop hiding or apologizing for who God created me to be. I needed to stop diminishing the gifts He has entrusted me with simply because it doesn't fit the status quo. And I bet if you were honest, you need a stage, too!

Maybe your stage is a person to disciple, a place to sow generously, a heart to mend, a child to raise, a business to start, a life to love, or a place to serve. I don't know what your "stage" is. But can we unashamedly admit this? We need it!!!

That stage needs you!!!

Please, dear friend, stop hiding and shrinking and trying to fit into a mold God didn't create for you! Discover your purpose and passions. Find the place you come alive. Find the people who draw out from the investment God has put inside of you! Step out from behind the curtain and be who and what God created you to be for the impact He has destined for this earth!

Find your "stage" and step on it often! You were made for this!!!

"Gracious words are a honeycomb, sweet to the soul and healing to the bones."
Proverbs 16:24 NIV

Do you feel like throwing in the towel?

Don't stop! Don't allow a moment to become a monument. We all have them. Those defeating, breathtaking, difficult, dark, deafening moments in life. Some are unforeseen, and others are self-inflicted.

The truth is both can be surrendered. Both can be sacrificed. And when we choose to sacrifice them on an altar of worship, we will inevitably see beauty rise from the ashes!

We know the promise that all things become new. We have heard the truth that purpose is produced from pain. But the fact is nothing can be resurrected until something is crucified.

Maybe today we need to crucify bitterness, unforgiveness, vengeance, retribution, the desire to understand or be understood, knowing the meaning or reason it happened like it did, the need to be right, justification, pride, a changing season...

I don't know what it is that you need to lay down. I am, however, painfully aware of the things in my own life that God is calling me to lay down, to sacrifice on His altar.

I'm not saying it is easy. But I am saying that His resurrection power is not lacking. When we are willing to embrace the sacrifice and see the ashes, we will most assuredly also see the promise of His beauty and power demonstrated as we see life come from death. Greatness will come from nothingness. Splendor will replace the stench of what used to be. The new will overtake the old.

And it will be ALL that God has spoken it to be!

"To all who mourn in Israel, he will give a crown of beauty for
ashes, a joyous blessing instead of mourning, festive praise instead of despair. In their righteousness, they will be like great oaks that the Lord has planted for his own."
Isaiah 61:3 NIV

Does your mind ever race when you desire to be still?

My days can be pretty busy. But this morning, I found myself awake, not in my usual rested state, but with a mind that seemed to have a mind of its own.

Thoughts, worries, plans – they were all swirling around, keeping me from the rest I needed. Instead of tossing and turning in bed, I made a decision. I slipped out of bed and tiptoed to my little office corner.

With a pen in hand, I poured out my thoughts onto paper. All those jumbled ideas and concerns found their place in the ink. And then, something beautiful happened. I prayed. With my hand on the page, I spoke life into every word I had written. I prayed for the people on my heart and for the situations weighing on my mind.

As I did, peace settled in the room. The chaos in my head quieted down, replaced by the calm assurance that God was taking care of it all.

You see, sometimes we try to figure everything out on our own, but we forget that our view is limited. When we bring our concerns to God, we open ourselves to His unlimited perspective and boundless love.

In His presence, the impossible loses its grip.

So, my friends, whatever you're facing today, I encourage you to follow suit. Take a moment, lay it all out before Him in prayer, and watch as peace replaces the turmoil. Keep your eyes on Him, for your help comes from the Lord, the Maker of heaven and earth.

What do you need to pen today, then boldly pray over and release into God's capable care?

"I lift up my eyes to the mountains— where does my help come from? My help comes from the LORD, the Maker of heaven and earth."
Psalm 121:1-2 NIV

Do you find yourself feeling depleted?

There are times in life when it seems like everything is being pulled away, leaving us feeling like the sandy shoreline before the next wave. We all encounter these seasons. They can leave us feeling empty, discouraged, and worn out.

These moments aren't the end of the story; they're a pause before a powerful wave of restoration crashes into our lives.

Imagine standing by the ocean, watching the water retreat before a new wave forms. You might feel like things are going backward or being taken away, but hold on tight – that's a sign that something bigger and better is about to come crashing in.

In the same way, when we feel depleted and drained, it's not time to walk away; it's time to hold on and wait for the wave of God's restoration.

Let's be real – waiting can be tough. But it's in these moments that our trust in God's promises truly shines.

Just like the wave follows the ebb of the ocean, God's joy is on its way to overtake your weariness.

And here's a secret: the harder the pull you're experiencing, the more massive the wave of joy coming.

When you're in this season, remember not to underestimate the power of worship. Your praise can determine the pace of the promise. So, while you're waiting, pour out your heart in worship, praise Him for His faithfulness, and watch how your praises become the rhythm of His promise in your life.

My fellow warrior, don't lose heart. Even when it feels like everything is being pulled away, know that God is preparing a wave of restoration that will sweep over your life. His promises are unwavering, His love is unchanging, and His joy will always follow the moments of pain. Hold on to His word, keep the faith, and watch as the tide turns in your favor.

"I consider that our present sufferings are not worth comparing with the glory that will be revealed in us."
Romans 8:18 NIV

Day 51

Can you have courage in the face of fear?

Can we talk about fear for a moment? I've been diving deep into this topic recently, and let's be honest, we all have a mix of rational and irrational fears, don't we? I mean, spiders? Yep, that's one for me. Not just the big, scary ones but even the tiny ones that somehow sneak into our homes during winter. (Don't even get me started on the jumping ones!) #irrationalfears, am I right? But here's the thing: it can't really hurt me, and deep down, I know that. Yet, the fear is real. (Note to self: probably shouldn't have watched Arachnophobia as a kid...)

Then, there are those rational fears, especially as a mom. Fears that hold weight, like the well-being of my family. These fears have real potential, the ones that keep us up at night. Health, finances, relationships—you name it. These #rationalfears are no joke.

But guess what? I've got a belief I want to share with you. We often hear about being "fearless," but honestly, that term doesn't quite fit the bill. It sounds like we need to eliminate all fear before moving forward in faith and power.

So, here's my preferred word:

COURAGEOUS! It means acknowledging the fear, feeling it, and then facing it head-on. That's courage, my friends. That's faith.

Instead of viewing fear as the enemy, what if we turned it into our greatest asset? For example, I'm so terrified of spiders that I'd sprint in the opposite direction.

Sometimes, we need to allow the fear of staying stagnant, the fear of not fulfilling our purpose and potential, to become the driving force propelling us into action!

How can you embrace your fears and channel them into courageous steps forward?

"For the Spirit God gave us does not make us timid, but gives us power, love and self-discipline."
2 Timothy 1:7 NIV

Do you realize you have irreplaceable value?

I remember hearing someone say once, "God does not love us equally. He loves us uniquely." Isn't that a comforting thought? It means we are not just a face in the crowd, lost in a sea of humanity.

No, we are intricately designed individuals, each with our own purpose and path.

Think about it: you're irreplaceable! Handcrafted by the Creator Himself, you hold a unique place in this world. There's a space in God's heart that only you can fill, a purpose that only you can fulfill. That's a truth we need to embrace and celebrate.

In a world that often tempts us to compare ourselves to others, remember this: **Your worth is immeasurable.**

You're not in competition with anyone else. You're not meant to be a replica of someone else's journey. You're on your own path, and that's a beautiful thing.

Embrace who you are today. Embrace the journey you're on. Be bold in claiming your unique worth. It's time to take back your joy, to live each day with a heart full of gratitude for the gift of being you.

Instead of looking around at others, let's look within.

Compare yourself to the person you were yesterday. Are you growing? Are you becoming a better version of yourself? That's the only comparison that truly matters.

Remember, the more rare and valuable something is, the higher its price. The same goes for you. Your uniqueness, your authenticity—they are your greatest assets. Own them proudly, for they define the beautiful tapestry of your life.

"For you created my inmost being; you knit me together in my mother's womb. I praise you because I am fearfully and wonderfully made; your works are wonderful, I know that full well."
Psalm 139:13-14 NIV

How do you embrace new beginnings?

Psalm 138 has truly shaken my heart this morning. I encourage you to read it! Have you ever stepped into a new season, a fresh chapter of life, feeling both exhilarated and anxious? The unknowns of new ventures can be both exciting and unsettling. Whether it's a budding relationship, a new job, uncharted territory in your marriage or family, or the awakening of a dormant passion, it's a mix of emotions that come with the territory. Perhaps you're seeking direction in your current phase of life.

Amidst all these uncertainties, let me offer you a challenge for today—worship. God's love for you is unyielding and unwavering. Have you ever paused to think that His perception of you remains unaltered by your self-perception?

It's easy to fall into the trap of thinking that God loves us despite our flaws, but the truth is that He loves us because of who we are and who He is.

No matter your past, your worries, or your mistakes, His love is steadfast. You were fashioned in the image of His love and created out of His boundless affection. The real question is, can you embrace that profound love for yourself?

Take a moment to worship, but approach it with the lens of His love for you. Worship not just because His promises are true, but because they are a reflection of His honorable nature. Know that the Lord is meticulously unfolding the blueprints of your life.

Trust the path, even when the progress isn't immediately apparent.

His love is eternal, and you, my friend, are an embodiment of that love. Keep enduring, for He walks beside you, every step of the way.

"And so we know and rely on the love God has for us. God is love. Whoever lives in love lives in God, and God in them."
1 John 4:16 NIV

How do you embrace new beginnings?

I lived in Chicago for 7 years and I can still vividly recall this beautiful morning. I gazed out of my bedroom window, watching the snow continue to fall, and it struck me how much life can mirror this scene. Here we are in Spring, yes you read that correctly.

Here we are in Spring and we still have all the signs and symptoms of winter. Doesn't that sound a lot like life? We enter a new season only to get discouraged that we are still experiencing the same signs and symptoms of the last one. It would be so easy to believe what we see and feel. I see snow falling and I feel frigid temps. It can feel as if winter will last forever.

Don't buy the lie of your circumstances. Spring has come. The promises of this new season are full of renewed life! You may still have a few snowy days, but flowers are just beneath the snowy surface waiting to bloom! Don't stop now.

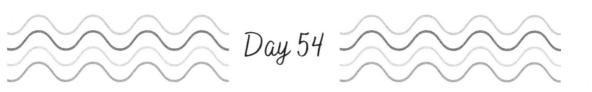

Warmer days are just ahead. Your symptoms will catch up with your season! Don't go into hibernation. Trust the process! The week prior we didn't have to wear coats, suddenly overnight we had to shovel snow.

When you feel like you took two steps forward and three steps back, don't quit!

Keep moving forward. Embrace each phase with the assurance that every setback is preparing you for a comeback. The snow will melt, the flowers will bloom, and the warmth will return. Just as nature reminds us, God is at work in every season, and there's a purpose to every moment.

Trust the process, hold on to hope, and keep moving forward. Spring is on the horizon, and it's brimming with promises waiting to unfold.

"Let us not become weary in doing good, for at the proper time we will reap a harvest if we do not give up."
Galatians 6:9 NIV

Day 55

How well do you rest?

Even Jesus, in all His divinity, took some time off to rest, reconnect to His Father, recharge, and be refreshed.

After a period of victory (Matthew 14:22)
Jesus had just experienced a significant moment of triumph, but He didn't dive right into the next task. He took some time for Himself.

When He needed to make a tough decision (Luke 6:12)
Jesus faced decisions just like we do, and He set an example by intentionally seeking a solitary place to pray. He understood that clarity often comes when we step away from the noise.

When He needed some alone time (Mark 7:24)
There were moments when Jesus withdrew from the crowds, even when demands were high. It's a reminder that finding solitude isn't a sign of weakness; it's a sign of self-care.

When He had an intimidating task on the horizon (Luke 22:41)

Even Jesus felt the weight of what was ahead. He retreated to pray before facing challenges. How incredible that He leaned into His connection with the Father during those moments.

What do you need to use time away for right now?

Maybe it's finding clarity, making a decision, recharging after a triumph, or preparing for a challenge. Whatever it is, remember that stepping back doesn't mean stepping down. It's a practice of self-care, a time to connect with God, and an investment in your overall well-being. If even Jesus knew the value of a retreat, we can surely follow His example too.

"Come to me, all you who are weary and burdened, and I will give you rest. Take my yoke upon you and learn from me, for I am gentle and humble in heart, and you will find rest for your souls. For my yoke is easy and my burden is light."
Matthew 11:28-30 NIV

What if fear is just misplaced faith?

By now, you know, I don't believe fear is the absence of faith. I believe it's more like a wayward cousin of faith. Fear is often faith's misguided counterfeit. The Bible tells us that we've all been given a measure of faith. Imagine it as this incredible gift from our Heavenly Father. But sometimes, instead of using that faith to anticipate the amazing, we let fear step in and distort our outlook.

Remember those words from Hebrews 11:1, "Faith is the substance of things hoped for and the evidence of things not seen"? That's gold! It's like having a pair of faith-powered glasses. What you see through them becomes the evidence of what you're believing for.

Ever noticed how worry, doubt, anxiety, and fear often tag along when we're looking at the unseen through negative lenses? But my friend, we have the power to switch the lens! We can turn our God-given faith towards good and positive outcomes.

So here's my encouragement for you today: believe the best.

Use that divine gift of faith to paint a picture of greatness in your mind. Envision God's plans unfolding, His provision overflowing, healing blossoming, and relationships mending.

You've got the choice – will you choose faith over fear?

Remember, fear might try to mimic faith, but its game is up. Choose to use your faith for something far greater – imagine the best, believe for greater things, and watch your perspective shift.

"So we say with confidence, 'The Lord is my helper; I will not be afraid. What can mere mortals do to me?'"
Hebrews 13:6 NIV

What is the price of your purpose?

Life has this funny way of teaching us valuable lessons, and recently, I've been reminded of the truth that to have value, there is first a price to be paid.

Have you ever read the story of Jesus feeding the 5,000 men not counting women and children with 5 loaves of bread and 2 fish. This story always reminds me that before something can be multiplied, it first needs to be blessed and then broken.

We all go through life experiences that shape us and refine us, preparing us to pour into the lives of others. It is in both blessing and breaking that we are multiplied.

But here's the thing – the process isn't always easy. Sometimes, it involves facing pain, struggles, and challenges that we'd rather sweep under the rug. We might be tempted to cover up our pain, put on a brave face, and pretend everything is fine.

Pain isn't meant to be covered; it's meant to communicate.

Just like our frustrations and discouragements can point to areas that need our attention, pain can speak to us as well. It's like a messenger trying to get our attention, telling us something needs healing or growth. Don't shy away from your pain or the challenges you face. Instead, let them be your guideposts, showing you the areas where growth is needed. Embrace the process, for in it lies the path to greater value, deeper understanding, and a more impactful life.

In the end, the cost we pay for growth and blessing is always worth it.

"For our light and momentary troubles are achieving for us an eternal glory that far outweighs them all. So we fix our eyes not on what is seen, but on what is unseen, since what is seen is temporary, but what is unseen is eternal."
2 Corinthians 4:17-18 NIV

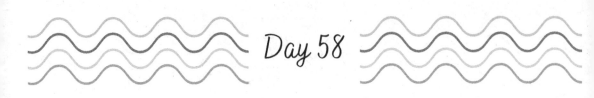

Have you considered the grace for your own growth?

It is truly amazing where some people survive, others can thrive. Have you ever noticed how something that brings one person down might actually catapult you to flight?

Admittedly I don't have a green thumb. But I have tried my hand at planting flowers over the years. The ones that begin to truly thrive often require a repotting and replanting to become all their potential demands of them.

Like those beautiful flowers, we're all unique, designed with a purpose that fits our individual journeys. So, what pulls them down into depression might be the very circumstance that lifts you from the depths of defeat.

There's no need to try to thrive in someone else's environment.

It's like trying to fit into a pot that's too small – you'll end up suffocating and starving. Just like our flowers that needed to be repotted to keep growing, sometimes we need a change of surroundings to truly flourish.

Day 58

So, embrace your repotting season. Don't be afraid to step into the place where you were designed to grow. It might not be comfortable at first, but it's where you'll truly thrive and bloom.

Just like those flowers needed a bigger pot to spread their roots, you might need to step out of your comfort zone to reach your full potential.

Remember, God has a unique plan for each of us, and He knows exactly where we'll flourish the most.

So, don't be afraid of change. Embrace it as an opportunity to grow and become everything you were meant to be.

"That person is like a tree planted by streams of water, which yields its fruit in season and whose leaf does not wither—whatever they do prospers."
Psalm 1:3 NIV

What is the speed of productivity?

Have you noticed how we wear busyness like a badge of honor? But let's be real – being constantly busy doesn't necessarily mean being productive. It's like a never-ending loop, where the more we have on our plate, the less we seem to accomplish. Sound familiar?

Here's the thing: nobody ever says, "I'm too productive to do this or that." Nope, it's always "I'm too busy." And trust me, friend, they're not the same thing. In fact, they're often worlds apart.

Picture this – you're spinning plates, juggling tasks, but deep down, there might be a little avoidance going on. Busyness can be our way of not truly facing what needs our attention. It's like we're running in circles, but avoiding the real destination.

Remember that you are designed for progress, not just motion. As daughters of faith, we're called to purposeful living, not frantic chaos. So, let's embrace the concept of slowing down with intention.

Think about it: when we pause, reflect, and prioritize, we often achieve more than when we're caught in the whirlwind of busyness.

Let's challenge the notion that busyness equals success. Let's break free from the cycle of frantic motion and allow ourselves to be intentional in our actions. Embrace those moments of stillness and reflection – those are the moments where true productivity and growth can flourish.

You're not just here to keep busy; you're here to make an impact, to bring light, and to make every moment count. So, let's slow down, breathe, and truly engage in purposeful living. Your journey is worth savoring, one intentional step at a time.

"Be still, and know that I am God."
Psalm 46:10 NIV

Was it growth or just favorable circumstances?

We all encounter pressure on our growth journeys. It has a way of revealing our true selves, shaking us from the comfort of the familiar, and nudging us to see if we've truly changed and grown, or if we've just been coasting on favorable circumstances.

Life's valleys, those times of pressure and challenge, might not be our favorite spots to linger, but they're like essential pit stops on the journey of becoming. Think about it like this: just as a butterfly needs its cocoon, we too need our cocoon moments of darkness, uncertainty, pressure and isolation to truly transform.

Imagine a caterpillar within its cocoon. During this hidden phase, it's not merely waiting; it's actively changing, rearranging, and evolving. The cocoon provides protection and darkness, allowing growth and transformation to happen unseen. In the same way, when life's pressures surround us, they serve as our cocoon.

Our hidden space to evolve, to strengthen our weaknesses, and to prepare us for the next stage.

Valleys, though daunting, are necessary. They provide a place of nourishment, a space to confront our weak points, and an opportunity to adapt.

You might not always see progress in the midst of pressure, but that's okay. Just as a caterpillar's transformation is hidden within its cocoon, your growth can sometimes be obscured by life's shadows.

But when those shadows lift, you'll emerge stronger, more resilient, and truly transformed.

"Not only so, but we also glory in our sufferings, because we know that suffering produces perseverance; perseverance, character; and character, hope."
Romans 5:3-4 NIV

Where Do We Find Our Strength?

Life truly is a divine journey, isn't it? As we walk this path, we realize that our beliefs, so deeply influenced by God's Word, have a profound way of shaping our world. Even when we face challenges, our choices reflect the depth of our faith and the love God has poured into our hearts.

Have you ever noticed those blessed moments where simple gestures - a child's innocent laughter, a kind word spoken in love, or a hand extended in fellowship - mirror God's love for us?

It's heartwarming to think that the true treasures we leave behind aren't just material possessions, but the spiritual lessons of hope, resilience, and love that we've learned from Scripture.

Throughout my conversations with many amazing people over the years, I've been reminded of a shared desire for understanding and a deep connection to God's promises.

The Bible tells us in James 1:2-3, "Consider it pure joy, my brothers and sisters, whenever you face trials of many kinds, because you know that the testing of your faith produces perseverance." Our life's journey, with its joys and tribulations, offers countless opportunities to grow closer to God.

And even amidst life's storms, we can find solace in the biblical truth that God is our refuge and strength.

So, as we face each day, let's do so with joyous hearts and an unwavering faith. After all, our personal testimonies and experiences might just be the beacon of hope and light someone else needs, reminding them of God's unwavering love.

"For this is the way the holy women of the past who put their hope in God used to adorn themselves. They submitted themselves to their own husbands..."
1 Peter 3:5

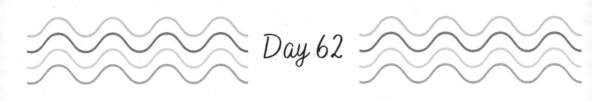

Where's Your Anchor?

Pull up a chair, grab a cup of coffee, because we've got some real talk to dive into. I have navigated some really challenging moments and seasons in my life. I've experienced abuse, lost a pregnancy, and lost both parents by the age of 37. I have been in the throws of marriage and parenting. I have served in ministry and scaled a business.

I've won and I've lost. But in it all, I have learned!

Life is this crazy, beautiful roller coaster, and sometimes it feels like you're holding on for dear life. But let's get something straight: the ups and downs? They're where we find our strength, our purpose, and yes, even our joy.

James 1:2-3 isn't just an inspiring verse; it's a life anthem for those of us who've danced with chaos and come out swinging. The storms of life, they're not stumbling blocks; they're stepping stones to something greater.

Now, I know what you might be thinking: "That's easier said than done." And hey, I hear you! But whether it's a family challenge, a business venture, or a personal goal, don't you dare underestimate the power of faith, hope, and a little sass to get you through.

Life's too short to shy away from our God-given potential.

So what do you say we rise up together? Let's embrace the chaos, laugh in the face of fear, and march forward with unshakable faith. Our destiny is calling, and trust me, it's worth every step, every struggle, every glorious victory.

"Consider it pure joy, my brothers and sisters, whenever you face trials of many kinds, because you know that the testing of your faith produces perseverance. Let perseverance finish its work so that you may be mature and complete, not lacking anything."
James 1:2-4 NIV

How do you find purpose in pain and live through loss?

Grief is a journey we all encounter at some point, a path of deep sorrow and longing for what once was. The loss of a dear friend or loved one, loss of a season gone, a business that's fallen, or the death of a dream can leave an emptiness that seems almost unbearable.

In the face of loss, daily responsibilities and celebrations continue. Life marches on, even when our hearts feel heavy. Can we be honest here? Sometimes, we may not feel like celebrating or giving. We may want to stop, sulk, hide, and cry. And that's okay. For a time.

Grief shouldn't be avoided, but it also shouldn't become our destination.

It's a process we walk with, feel, embrace, and move forward with, but not away from. It's allowing ourselves to feel the pain but also to let God give that pain purpose.

In our moments of remembrance and sorrow, gratitude can also find its place.

Day 63

We can be thankful for the time we had, the memories shared, and the faith that sustains us. We can recognize the beauty in the pain, understanding that life is indeed short, and our days are not promised. This realization calls us to live with purpose and passion.

If grief teaches us anything, it's that our lives are our testimony. Every single day, we have the opportunity to impact this world with kindness, love, and God's goodness. Give, even when you're grieving. Embrace the memories. Don't avoid the pain. Let God build something beautiful in this season of your life.

One of the ways I have found to navigate loss is to give while grieving or serve in sorrow.

This, for me, is how I choose to live out a legacy and honor those we miss or the seasons that are now gone. And in doing so, we find a strength and a hope that anchors us, not only in our loss but in our love, faith, and commitment to live fully, every single day.

"A generous person will prosper; whoever refreshes others will be refreshed."
Proverbs 11:25 NIV

Grasshopper Vision - Step one: Perspective and Potential

Perspective is powerful! Think about the Israelites, wandering for 40 years on what should have been an 11-day journey to their promised land flowing with milk and honey. I know, it's easy to get impatient with their story. It's even easy to critizize the group who saw God's demonstrated promises first hand and still chose to grumble and complain along the journey.

But then I remember my own propensity to grumble and complain when things aren't happening how I want and when I want. I find myself becoming impatient and if I'm not careful I can do my fair share of grumbling and complaining. Can you relate? It's not just about the destination but the journey.

How are we choosing to think, act, and speak on the way to our own promises being fulfilled? With gratitude or grumbling?

Whether it's motherhood, entrepreneurship, or just trying to follow Jesus, we can get caught in a loop of our past and forget our potential.

So today, what old habits are holding you back? What God-given potential have you not yet awakened?

Let's dare to believe, dare to dream, and dare to think differently, just like Joshua and Caleb. They were the only two of twelve who went ahead to take a peek at what was possible and came back with a different report. They took one look and where others saw problems they saw potential. When the rest saw obstacles, they saw opportunity! They chose to see the land through the lens of how big their God was rather than how big the giants were.

It's time to rise up, change your perspective, and step into your promised land.

"We saw the giants there, and we felt like grasshoppers. And that's what we looked like to them."
Numbers 13:33 NIV

Grasshopper Vision – Step Two: Embracing Change

How many of us carry our old mindsets and habits that no longer serve us? They are like an unwanted song stuck on repeat? It is this never ending cylce that just won't break? Change is a process, not a moment, and it's a process that requires faith.

The Israelites had witnessed miracles, but they were still stuck in their slave mentality. I've experienced that too.

I have been the recipient of God's healing power. I was extremely sick in 2013 and had an undiagnosed disorder that left me completely blind in both eyes with no hope of recovering my sight.

But God! Amidst experiencing my own miracles, I still wage war against old thought patterns that still seek to imprison me to past beliefs.

Are you still viewing new opportunities through an old lens?

What is the last miracle you watched God perform in your life? You know what I'm talking about. That last thing you throught would crush you but somehow you survived.

Keep that in mind as you look ahead with expectancy! The majority around you may choose negativity and complaining. They may only see the problems.

But you've been given the vision to see the potential!!

Don't be afraid to wage war against the status quo and choose to believe that with God, all things are possible!

"For I know the plans I have for you," declares the LORD, "plans to prosper you and not to harm you, plans to give you hope and a future."
Jeremiah 29:11

Grasshopper Vision – Step Three: Seeing Beyond Limitations

Have you ever stood before a mirror, gazing at your reflection, and sensed the weight of self-imposed limitations pressing upon you until you felt like you were being suffocated?

It's a sentiment that resonates with many, one that even the Israelites once grappled with. Remarkably, the Bible recounts how they perceived themselves as insignificant grasshoppers, imprisoned by their own self-image.

What's intriguing is that their confinement wasn't solely a product of external judgments but was predominantly rooted in their own perceptions. So, how do you perceive yourself when you gaze into the mirror of self-reflection?

It's crucial to engrave this truth deep within your heart: the labels you wear and the errors of the past do not possess the power to define your intrinsic worth.

It's an imperative that we realize that our history, whether embellished with failures or adorned with successes, should not become the shackles that restrain us.

We possess the extraordinary capability to peer beyond the boundaries of our self-imposed limitations and entrust our destinies to the unwavering sovereignty of God's divine plan.

Remember, your history may narrate the path you've taken, but it does not have to dictate the course of your future!

Instead, it is your unshakable faith and relentless perseverance that propel you forward, illuminating the path toward triumphant destiny. It's time to break free from those self-imposed chains, embrace your full potential, and let your faith lead you to a future filled with endless possibilities. You're made for greatness!

"For I know the plans I have for you," declares the LORD, "plans to prosper you and not to harm you, plans to give you hope and a future."
Jeremiah 29:11 NIV

Grasshopper Vision – Step Four: Daring to Be Different

Have you ever felt the urge to dare to be different? Two men in history did, and they changed their destiny. Joshua and Caleb were not afraid of giants; they saw the promise, not the problem. That's the spirit we all need to cultivate.

Life is filled with challenges, be it health issues, building a business, or raising a family. Each of us faces our own "giants."

But the question is, what will we dare to do differently? How will we rise above?

Just like Caleb and Joshua, we must speak faith over fear, potential over problems, and promises over perceptions. We are called to awaken to our God-given purpose and lead with conviction and courage.

It's not about following the crowd; it's about following the call.

Let's be bold and unapologetic about who we are and what we believe in. The world needs your voice, your gifts, and your faith.

Embrace the difference, face the day with unwavering passion, and know that you, my friend, are destined for greatness.

Rise up, take the path less traveled, and watch how God transforms your life. You are meant to shine, and your time is now.

"Have I not commanded you? Be strong and courageous. Do not be afraid; do not be discouraged, for the LORD your God will be with you wherever you go."
Joshua 1:9 NIV

Unshakeable Peace in Life's Storms

You know, life's storms can come at us with ferocity, can't they? It's in those moments that we desperately need something unshakable, something strong.

Today, I feel this burning desire to lead you to the irrevocable peace of God. It's right there in the middle of your storm. And guess what? God's not going back on this promise.

Let's breathe it in together. Deep, deep breaths. That's the life-sustaining force of God's love. Can you feel it?

Focus now, not on the winds and the waves but on the God who clothes even the flowers and nourishes the birds every single day. His love for you? It's a boundless ocean and it's time to drink in His peace.

The peace of God literally guards your heart and mind. That's what the Bible says! It is your shield.

Day 68

Are you ready to dance through the rain?

To defy the storm with the gift of His peace? It's like tasting the richest coffee, prepared specially for you by the Creator of the universe.

I've seen storms, and I've felt the wind. I've tasted fear and worry. But I've also tasted victory. Because I've learned to cling to that unbreakable peace of God. It's not a fleeting emotion; it's an unshakable truth.

Dear friends, let's walk into our storms, not with trepidation but with faith. Let's trust in His provision. No storm is too big, no wave too high, no wind too strong for our God. He's got you.

How can you, right now, in the midst of your storm, step into His peace? His love is reaching out to you. Will you take it? Reflect on His love, embrace His unshakable peace today. Let it change you, fuel you, and empower you to overcome!

"And the peace of God, which transcends all understanding, will guard your hearts and your minds in Christ Jesus."
Philippians 4:7

Do you have resilience?

"But I am like an olive tree FLOURISHING in the house of God; I trust in God's unfailing love for ever and ever."
Psalm 52:8

This is beautiful biblical imagery of who God created you to be! What is it about the olive tree that makes it so special?

The olive tree is more than a symbol; it's a powerful example of strength, resilience, and vitality.

Olive trees, with their gnarled trunks and sprawling branches, aren't just beautiful to look at. They're warriors! Equipped to handle subzero temperatures, droughts, frost, and even fire, these trees stand as a testament to endurance. Just like you, these trees have been through the storms of life, but they don't give up; they stand firm, rooted in the soil of faith.

Their extraordinary resilience reminds me of the journey many of us face, especially as we navigate the complex paths of life.

The roots of the olive tree are something to marvel at; they're so strong that the tree can regrow even when it seems to have been completely decimated. Can't you see the divine parallel here?

Even when we feel cut down, broken, and lost, our roots in Christ allow us to regrow, to flourish again. We are anchored in His love, a love that never fails. If God can cause an olive tree to thrive despite the harshest conditions, how much more will He enable us to flourish in His house?

Stand strong, resilient, and faithful. Grow, not in spite of our trials but because of them. Trust in God's unfailing love, knowing that we are called to flourish, not merely survive.

Just as the olive tree bears fruit in it's season despite all it has been through, so will you. Drink in that truth today, and let it nourish your soul. You were made to flourish!

"And let us not grow weary of doing good, for in due season we will reap, if we do not give up."
Galatians 6:9 ESV

The Lion's Perspective - Seeing Opportunities, Not Opposition

Who told the lion he was the king of the jungle? Have you ever wondered about that? He's not the largest or the most powerful, but there's something about him that sets him apart.

It's his attitude, his unwavering conviction.

When he looks at the elephant, he doesn't see a bigger opponent; he sees a bigger opportunity, a bigger feast.

What if we chose to have a lion mentality?

We're often faced with what seems like insurmountable opposition. When faced with a challenge we often look at it, and all we see is something bigger, something scarier. But what if we shift our perspective?

Just like the lion, we can choose to see our challenges not as opposition but as opportunity.

With God's wisdom, we understand that "As a man thinketh in his heart, so is he" (Proverbs 23:7).

Our mindset shapes our reality.

We can be strong and courageous, for the LORD our God is with us wherever we go (Joshua 1:9).

So take a moment and look again!

Look with the eyes of faith. Look with the heart of a conqueror. Look with the attitude of a lion. You're called to be the king or queen of your domain.

Remember the lion's perspective: It's not about being bigger; it's about being bolder. Embrace that lion's attitude today and watch how your life begins to flourish. You can laugh in the face of adversity, knowing that you've got a God who's more significant than any challenge.

"But you are a chosen people, a royal priesthood, a holy nation, God's special possession, that you may declare the praises of him who called you out of darkness into his wonderful light."
1 Peter 2:9 NIV

What does the word "freedom" mean to you?

I have the sweetest little chihuahua named Lacey. One night I could hear her pitifully crying in her cage, desperately wanting to get out. With a heavy heart, I walked downstairs only to find that her cage door was never actually latched.

Lacey was free the whole time, but she was so accustomed to her cage being locked when she was inside that she believed she was trapped. She saw familiar conditions and never even imagined the outcome could be completely different. So much so, she didn't even attempt to come out.

Isn't that a profound lesson for all of us? Sometimes we, too, believe we are confined to our present circumstances, not realizing that we are free to break out any time we desire.

The story you tell yourself matters. Imagining where you want to be, not just where you hope to be, is essential. If you can picture it, see yourself there, and play it like a movie in your mind, your emotions will attach to that story.

This is so vital to understand because your brain doesn't know how to differentiate between the story you're telling and the reality you're living. Ever cried during a movie or jumped during a scary scene? That story wasn't real, but how you felt was.

In the same way, the stories we tell ourselves can become our reality.

They can either imprison us like Lacey in her unlatched cage or empower us to chase after the life we're meant to live.

Your prison doors have already been opened.

So today, live like you're already free! Choose to tell yourself stories filled with faith, hope, courage, and love. Embrace the truth that we are indeed free, and we have the power to shape our destinies. Hold onto God's promise, and let's step into the life we've imagined, knowing we are already free!

"So if the Son sets you free, you will be free indeed."
John 8:36 NIV

How do you rise from rejection?

Rejection is a universal human experience. No one is immune from its sting, whether it's a job we didn't get, a friend who drifts away, or a failure that feels like it defines us. But, oh, the beauty of rising up from rejection!

The story of triumph is often found in the heartache of what seems like failure.

The Bible tells us in 2 Corinthians 4:9, "But he said to me, "My grace is sufficient for you, for my power is made perfect in weakness." Therefore I will boast all the more gladly of my weaknesses, so that the power of Christ may rest upon me."

God already knew we would experience the dissapointment and frustration of rejection if we are in pursuit of a God sized dream and impact.

But there are many successful leaders who have forged paths that we can learn from.

Just look at Michael Jordan, who has missed more than 9,000 shots in his career. He's lost almost 300 games. He was even cut from his high school basketball team!

But did he give up? No! He once said, "I have failed over and over and over again in my life. And that is why I succeed."

Rejection didn't define him; his persistence did.

Consider Thomas Edison and his quest to invent the lightbulb. Over a thousand failed attempts, but he never gave up. He famously said, "I have not failed. I've just found 10,000 ways that won't work."

We don't remember the failures; we celebrate the success that lights our way.

You may have been knocked down but you get the choice to stay there or to rise up and choose today to START AGAIN!

But you, take courage! Do not let your hands be weak, for your work shall be rewarded."
2 Chronicles 15:7

Are you willing to suffer for a little while?

The Bible is full of stories of rejection too. Jesus, our Savior, faced rejection in His hometown and by those closest to Him. He started with a multitude, but only 12 remained.

In John 6:66, many of his disciples turned back and no longer followed Him. But those 12 who stayed? They have changed the entire world every generation since.

The rejection became the platform for a global transformation.

The Apostle Paul, too, knew rejection. In 2 Corinthians 4:8-9, he writes, "We are hard-pressed on every side, but not crushed; perplexed, but not in despair; persecuted, but not abandoned; struck down, but not destroyed."

His faith carried him through the rejections and into a legacy of faith that continues to inspire us today.

So, friend, whatever rejection you are facing, know this: Your victory is on the other side. Rise up! Press on! For God promises in Romans 8:28 that all things work together for good for those who love Him.

The rejection you face today might just be the path to the success you will embrace tomorrow.

Just like Jordan and Edison your story isn't defined by the times you fell, but by the grace and determination with which you rise.

Jesus was the greatest example of all turning rejection into triumph. So embrace this season, knowing that you're in good company. Lean into God, trust His plan, and know that He's crafting your story into something beautiful.

Rise up! Your victory awaits! May what you feel despised for become what you are known for!

"I press on toward the goal to win the prize for which God has called me heavenward in Christ Jesus."
Philippians 3:14 NIV

You will see what you say!

Let's take a moment to reflect on the words we're speaking into our lives. Are we claiming God's promises? Or are we letting the whispers and judgments of others define us? The power in the Word of God is extraordinary; it's alive, it's vibrant, and it's yours to use.

When you speak His word, it carries the same weight, the same authority as when it comes from His very lips.

Don't you dare let anyone else's words become your compass! You know who you are in Christ. His breath is in your lungs, and that same breath, that God-breath, should be what guides your words, your actions, and your heart.

Intentionally speak His truth over yourself, and let His word become your identity.

Now, here's a truth that might sting a little: there's nothing sadder than seeing someone live their entire life, bound and broken by the words of others, never fully embracing their God-given identity. They were meant for greatness, destined for a purpose, but they've allowed the influence of others to guide them. Don't be that person.

Stand tall and speak life. Embrace the life He's designed for you.

Reclaim your identity in Christ, and don't let anyone or anything else dictate your worth. Remember Isaiah 55:11 – His Word will not return void. It has to land somewhere.

Allow His word to land in your heart, and watch the transformative power it brings to your life!

"But you are a chosen people, a royal priesthood, a holy nation, God's special possession, that you may declare the praises of him who called you out of darkness into his wonderful light."
1 Peter 2:9 NIV

Ever feel like you're caught in an unending cycle of trials?

As if you are barely catching your breath before the next wave of adversity crashes over you? Oh, I've been there too. Those are the moments where it feels like you're drowning in the sorrows of life, like your lungs are filling with water and escape is an illusion.

You're trying everything possible, flailing about just to stay afloat.

I'm a beach baby at heart; the ocean calls my name! If you want to see me at my best, take me to the ocean! I vividly remember vacations as a child with salt in the air, the sun on my skin, and those huge, crashing waves in my sights. As beautiful as they are, they can also be dangerous.

Isn't life a series of waves, sometimes crashing one after the other, giving us barely enough time to catch our breath. But here's the kicker: even in the fury of life's storms, you have a choice—to keep struggling or to find another way.

Even though my childhood family vacations always included the beach, my dad was not a water guy at all. Yet,out of necessity he found himself in the ocean trying to rescue a friend who was pulled out too far. He was fighting its pull, thinking he could swim his way out of it. And just when he thought he couldn't take it anymore, he did something counterintuitive. He took a breath. One big, life-changing breath that allowed him to float rather than fight.

Sometimes, the best thing you can do is to stop fighting, take a breather, and let the wave carry you.

Because, trust me, sometimes surrendering to the flow isn't giving up; it's choosing a different kind of strength. It's about knowing when to work hard and when to rest in the power that's greater than us. So what's that situation you're trying to control? Maybe it's time to just let go and let the waves guide you back to safety.

"Commit your way to the Lord; trust in Him, and He will act."
Psalm 37:5 ESV

Is fear your constant companion?

I've been in this place. When it's the first voice you hear in the morning and the last one you hear at night? You're not alone. But here's a game-changer:

It's not about the storm that's raging around you; it's about what you let into your heart and soul that'll sink you.

So, be vigilant. Guard your atmosphere like your life depends on it—because it does. Imagine your soul like a ship. A ship isn't threatened by the water around it; it's only when water gets inside that it starts to sink.

Do you catch my drift?
We have a choice, a divine privilege, to keep our soul's ship watertight. Fear might be raging like a tempest around you, but you don't have to let it inside.

No, not today, not on your watch! Boot out that fear. Set up the spiritual sump pump and start bailing, because you have been empowered for more.

Look, if you're the captain, then stand at the helm of your life and make a declaration: "No unauthorized items on board!"

Guard your heart fiercely. Secure your soul's hatches. You have authority over what gains entry—exercise it.

I want you to sail, not sink. We're all facing storms; that's life. But not all of us have to let the storms inside. Today, let's choose faith over fear. You're more resilient than you think; you've got more fight in you than you realize.

Rise up, guard your atmosphere, and watch how you weather any storm life throws your way.

"The Sovereign LORD is my strength; he makes my feet like the feet of a deer, he enables me to tread on the heights."
Habakkuk 3:9 NIV

What storm have you been asking God to deliver you from?

Today you might be begging God to yank you out of your storm, but what if He has something greater in mind? The Bible contains a few great examples we can glean from.

Jonah in that giant fish, Shadrach, Meshach, and Abednego sizzling in the furnace, and Daniel cozying up with lions. None of them got a get-out-of-jail-free card. Instead, God rolled up His sleeves and got right in there with them!

We want the miracle of God delivering us *from* the storm, but often, the bigger miracle is Him delivering us *in* the storm.

What if God is writing your greatest life chapters in the middle of your toughest storms? Transformation is happening, my friend. Probably the very kind you've prayed for and it's not the kind you can fast-forward through.

I get it. The storm is raging, and it's scary. The fire's intense, and those lions aren't purring. But, listen, the moment you think you're sinking is the very moment God's doing His finest work in you. Imagine the spiritual muscle you're gaining, trudging through the gale, enduring the heat, facing the roar!

I've been there, we all have, asking, "God, where are you?" And guess what? He's saying, "I'm right here, doing something in you that calm waters could never achieve."

You see, God's not in the business of evacuation; He's in the business of transformation.

So if you're feeling overwhelmed, remember: you're not forsaken; you're being formed. Just like our Bible heroes, your storm isn't a setback; it's a setup for God to show up and show off in ways you never even thought possible. So lean in, my friend. This storm might just become your greatest testimony yet!

"For our light and momentary troubles are achieving for us an eternal glory that far outweighs them all."
2 Corinthians 4:17 NIV

Does it ever feel too heavy to carry?

Here's the invitation. Every sunrise God whispers to us, "Bring it all to me—the good, the bad, and everything in between." This isn't your run-of-the-mill morning ritual. Psalm 5:3 is all about vulnerability, about laying every piece of your life on God's altar—your hopes, your dreams, your fears, even your disappointments.

With God, you don't have to put on a brave face; you can bring your raw, unfiltered self.

Let's face it, life can sometimes feel like a constant battle, and you might be tempted to wear your armor 24/7. But God's asking for your vulnerability. It's an audacious kind of faith, a faith that says, "Here's all of me, Lord—every broken piece, every unfulfilled dream."

And you know what happens when we do this? We wait, full of anticipation for His fire to fall upon us. The kind of that refines but also refreshes. The kind that burns away but also burns within. Its the kind of blaze that can be trusted.

We offer Him our openness, our vulnerabilities, and He infuses us with His divine strength. It's life-altering! It's trustworthy.

That moment of surrender, that's when we experience a closeness to God that sets our souls on fire!

Remember, when we're vulnerable before God, He makes beauty out of our brokenness. All of it, every shard, is turned into something breathtaking and remarkable under His divine touch.

So tomorrow morning, before reaching for your phone, reach out to God. Lay all of yourself on His altar—the highs, the lows, every fragment—and wait for His fire to fall. When you do, you'll find that He takes even the most shattered pieces and creates a masterpiece. Prepare to be amazed!

"At each and every sunrise you will hear my voice as I prepare my sacrifice of prayer to you. Every morning I lay out the pieces of my life on the altar and wait for your fire to fall upon my heart."
Psalm 5:3 TPT

Are you tired or weary?

We've all said it— "I'm just so tired." But let's be real; there's a world of difference between being tired and being weary. If you're tired, a power nap or a good night's sleep can perk you right up. But weariness? Oh, that's a whole other animal, trust me!

You see, when you're weary, your soul needs more than just a timeout.

It needs a recharge, a renewal that runs deeper than a quick snooze could ever offer. It's like running on fumes in a car; what you need isn't just a pit stop, but a full-on tank refill.

So, what's the game plan when weariness sets in?

First, pinpoint what's draining you. Is it a toxic relationship, an unfulfilling job, a loss, a long lasting difficulty, or maybe you're spiritually parched?

Identify it, and then take it straight to God. Yes, in those soul-deep weary moments, it's time to get down on your knees and have a real, raw conversation with your Heavenly Father.

Because, guess what? He specializes in reviving the weary.

He's in the business of renewing your spirit, refreshing your soul, and refilling your empty tank. It's like divine caffeine for the soul!

Let's shake off that weariness by plugging into the ultimate Source of renewal. You're not just tired; you're weary. And in your weariness, allow God to refresh you from the inside out. Trust me, that's when the true, life-altering revitalization begins!

"You, God, are my God, earnestly I seek you; I thirst for you, my whole being longs for you, in a dry and parched land where there is no water."
Psalm 63:1 NIV

Day 80

What do you need to stop apologizing for?

I talk with people regularly who have such a desire for more. Yet, almost all of them also feel the need to apologize for that desire. Afraid, unsure, intimidated, feeling unqualified and unworthy, we often bow out gracefully from pursuing our dreams.

Have you ever stopped to consider that your dreams are by design? Did it ever occur to you that your dreams were God's first? We are created in the image of our Father. He is the ultimate creator and designer of dreams. Before it could be imagined in your mind, it had to be imagined in His. If you are sensing the desire for more, could that be a download from the one who made you?

If we believe that to be true, don't wait on fear and feelings to leave. Those things tend to show up no matter where you find yourself.

Fear may be present for the ride, but I refuse to allow it in the driver's seat!

Maybe it's time to start talking back to the fear and feelings of insecurity and inadequacy that so loudly talk to us! Maybe we should start this way, "You better hope you can keep up because I'm about to start running full speed after my dreams, destiny, and design! So you'll have to find me to speak to me. I'll be vacating this spot of comfort and complacency with or without you!"

Get up and get going!!! The impact on the other side of your decision is the very reason fear is trying to hold you back in the first place!

Rise up and Run! I'll just be over here cheering you on!!!

As for us, we have all of these great witnesses who encircle us like clouds. So we must let go of every wound that has pierced us and the sin we so easily fall into. Then we will be able to run life's marathon race with passion and determination, for the path has been already marked out before us.
Hebrews 12:1 TPT

Are you ready to grow your GRIT muscle?

This is for you, my fellow fire-starters, trailblazers, holy hustlers, and world-changers! Listen up because I've got a paradigm shift of epic proportions. We all know the drill: work hard, persevere, and you'll eventually get where you want to be, right? One definition of grit is summed up as passion and perseverance for the long haul. But what happens when you feel unable to keep it up? There's another layer to this —

I'm talking about Grit, God's Way!

I know you're juggling a million things: family, work, personal growth, and heck, just the daily grind of life. You're stretched thinner than a guitar string, and still, you're supposed to have the grit to just keep plucking along? It just doesn't work that way. We need something sustainable, something eternal! That's where Grit, God's Way comes in.

What's the secret? God! It is the grit we gain and grow when we allow Him to set the pace, the goals, and the strategy. Dive in with me for the next 90 days to shift your perspective, catch your breath, renew your passion, and set ablaze the fire in your heart and soul that may have dwindled! This is a divine invitation to grow your grit, God's Way!

Day 81

Those moments with God are my daily bookends and I want you to use them, too!

Why? Because when you let God steer your grit, you're not just chasing after dreams; you're chasing after His Kingdom. That's right, Kingdom impact, baby! You're not just fueling your stamina with earthly moxie; you're fueling it with celestial power!

That's the kind of grit that doesn't just endure; it conquers!

So let's redefine grit, not as a worldly badge of honor, but as a heavenly mantle of purpose!

Grit, God's Way is the relentless pursuit of Kingdom impact, fueled by God-given strength, stamina, and strategy.

So gear up, aim high, and let's do this — God's Way!

"Not by might nor by power, but by my Spirit," says the LORD Almighty."
Zechariah 4:6 NIV

Do you want to conquor your day?

Every morning, start with an attitude of gratitude. Ephesians 5:20 is not just about a spiritual high-five to the sky, it's an activated lifestyle choice that—even science, yes neuroscience, corroborates! Can you believe it?

Here's the 101. Each morning, jot down five one-of-a-kind God moments. No repeats allowed! This isn't just a 'feel-good' exercise; you're actually recalibrating your brain and giving it marching orders on what you want it to seek out through the day. Yeah, you heard me right. You're instructing your brain to be on constant lookout for God's blessings, like you're a scout on a divine assignment.

Don't rush past this. Truly marinate in those moments you've written down. Feel that joy surge through you again. Why? Because you're releasing your brain's very own 'feel good' chemicals. Dopamine, serotonin, you name it!

This isn't just about emotion, this is physiological and spiritual transformation happening right there!

Even in the messiest chapters of your life story, this practice digs out gems you'd otherwise miss. It's like mining for gold in the middle of the mud.

You find lessons enveloped in trials and grace glinting through the grime.

That's not just resilience; that's Kingdom-grade, Holy Spirit-filled grit. Make this your daily anthem. Because gratitude isn't just a warm fuzzy; it's spiritual warfare. You're aligning your very neurons with heaven's frequency.

This is not just coping; this is conquering.

So take charge, unleash that God-graced grit and let's live with a seismic gratitude that shakes heaven and earth. This is how we rise, this is how we thrive, this is how we become unstoppable!

"Always giving thanks to God the Father for everything, in the name of our Lord Jesus Christ."
Ephesians 5:20 NIV

What's the last revelation you had?

So often we sail right past these precious revelation moments rather than truly reflecting on them and extracting every ounce of goodness God packed them with upon delivery.

That is about to change because I've stumbled upon a life-changing practice that'll supercharge your spiritual journey! It's all about seizing those 'Aha' moments with God. Each morning, I grab my journal and jot down a scripture that's rocking my world right now.

It's not just about the words; it's about how God uses those ancient lines to direct my hustle today.

Why settle for a surface-level faith when you can dig deeper? Write down those revelations and nuggets of wisdom you sense God pouring into your spirit. Trust me, God is always speaking; the question is, are we listening?

And let's not forget the mirror effect. When you see yourself through His eyes, it's life-altering!

Ask yourself: What am I learning about God today? What am I learning about myself in His magnificent mirror? The answers are bound to shake your world.

A piece of paper can't contain the fullness of the living, breathing Word of God, but writing it down helps etch it onto the tablet of your heart. Don't have a routine of devotion? No problem. Just pick a verse that hits you hard and write it down. Let it sink into the core of who you are.

This isn't religious obligation, my friends, it's a divine invitation!

You know how everyone's talking about 'mindfulness'? Well, I'm here to tell you that the best kind of mindfulness comes when you meditate on His Word.nAs you step into your day, this practice equips you with heaven's perspective. It's not just about facing the day; it's about conquering it with kingdom insight. Let's make this a non-negotiable habit and watch how God shows up!

"But whose delight is in the law of the Lord, and who meditates on his law day and night."
Psalm 1:2 NIV

Who do you say that I AM?

Did you know that you're bombarded by between 12,000 to 60,000 thoughts a day? And get this—most of them are negative reruns from yesterday! It's high time we disrupt this thought pattern and shatter the cycle!

The most potent words you can ever utter are "I am."

Yep, just two words! But what follows these words will either make or break you. We've let the world, our past, even our own limiting beliefs complete that sentence for us for far too long!

Stop settling for an identity handed to you by life's circumstances or other people's perceptions.

Instead, get grounded in who you are in Christ, and watch how your life begins to transform. If you dive into the research, the science is actually there to back this up!

So, here's your homework: Write down five affirmations that resonate with the truest, most authentic you. Perhaps you need to identify the lies that you've believed and unveil the truth of the word and claim that identity as yours! Speak these out loud daily—yes, out loud!

There's power in giving voice to your identity.

When you're anchored in who you are and Whose you are, you're unstoppable! Now you're ready to make an IMPACT from your identity in Christ! Maybe you won't change the whole world overnight, but each day you have the power and opportunity to change someone's world!

Focusing on impact swings your compass back to your true north—your purpose. And let me tell you, that's where real fulfillment starts simmering and ultimately boils over! So, what are you waiting for? Get out there and be the 'I AM' you were created to be!

"Above all else, guard your heart, for everything you do flows from it."
Proverbs 4:23 NIV

"Are You Targeting Your Day or Letting Triggers Target You?"

If you want to nail this day, you've gotta get laser-focused on your target—just like Jesus did! I'm talking about that one thing that will make or break your day, that thing that will set your soul on fire! You won't be able to do everything and too often that stops us from doing something or the one thing that is most important!

Now write it down! No, seriously, WRITE. IT. DOWN. This is your North Star for the day, your ticket to feeling like you crushed it!

But here's the kicker: *targets* come with *triggers*.

You know what I'm talking about—those pesky obstacles, interruptions, and naysayers that try to sidetrack you. So let's get smart and anticipate those triggers.

What might throw you off course today? Is it that co-worker who loves to gossip? The unexpected errands that always pop up? Identify them. Write those down too!

Don't stop there. Close your eyes and envision how your best self would tackle those triggers. See yourself navigating through them like a boss! How would you in 10 years navigate those same circumstances? Would you be easily angered or calm and forgiving?

Nothing is stopping you from choosing to respond today with that amount of wisdom, experience, maturity, and grace.

This is your call to action to keep your eyes so locked on that target that the triggers don't stand a chance. Make your day significant by setting your gaze on what matters most.

"[Looking away from all that will distract us and] focusing our eyes on Jesus, who is the Author and Perfecter of faith [the first incentive for our belief and the One who brings our faith to maturity], who for the joy [of accomplishing the goal] set before Him endured the cross, disregarding the shame, and sat down at the right hand of the throne of God [revealing His deity, His authority, and the completion of His work]."
Hebrews 12:2 AMP

When does your grit have grace?

If we are honest, we're all in some serious need of grace, aren't we? Whether it's the grace to navigate our imperfections or the grace to extend toward others when they, in all their human glory, irritate the living daylights out of us. We're all in this holy hustle together. Let's start by admitting something that could feel like a weakness but is actually a God-given strength—our need for grace.

God's grace isn't just sufficient; it's an over-the-top, soul-quenching, heart-pounding reality that takes us from being merely human to fully alive!

Instead of lamenting over our weaknesses, let's BOAST in them, because that's when His power perfects itself in us. We're not just receiving grace; we're marinating in it.

It's as if God's saying, "I've got you. Even when you think you're falling apart, I'm piecing you together in ways you can't even imagine."

We don't stop at receiving this grace. We extend it. Your family, your friends, that irritating barista—they need it too. We've all been cut off in traffic, hurt by people we love, or felt the bitter sting of betrayal. It's easy to point fingers, but you've got moments of humanity too, don't you? That's why we need to start with Part 1. Take another deep dive if you need to. Marinate some more in God's grace before you go sprinkling it around.

Because here's the deal: when you get Part 1 right, Part 2 becomes a piece of cake—or should I say, a drink of living water? We've got to pour out what we've been filled with. It's time to be conduits of His grace, not reservoirs.

So, get in the presence of the Lord. Picture holding those offenses, that anger, those disappointments in your hands. Now, let it go. Drop it. Surrender it all at the feet of Jesus, where grace flows like a river. Pray this prayer with me: "Lord, love them through me, as me." Because, let's be honest, sometimes we can't love them on our own. But with God's grace we become unstoppable fountains of His love.

"But by the grace of God I am what I am, and his grace to me was not without effect."
1 Corinthians 15:10 NIV

What do you need to release to rest?

You know how it feels when the day winds down and you're staring at that to-do list, right? Almost like you're in a staring contest, except your list isn't blinking. If you're anything like me, you can feel a bit defeated, as if you've somehow lost a battle with time itself. Well, let's change the narrative.

You see, I've learned that at the end of the day, it's not about how many boxes I've checked off, but about accepting the boxes I did manage to check and releasing what I didn't. When you've given your all, that's when you can release. Yep, you heard me—release it. Let it go, Elsa style, and hand it over to God.

Have you ever heard that saying, "Don't bring your work home with you?" Well, don't bring your day into your night either. You need your rest, spiritually and physically. I always remember what an incredible coach once said to me: "Pass the baton at the end of the day."

Like a team marathon runner, we don't run this race alone! Give it to God and let Him take the night shift.

He's the ultimate multitasker, working things out even while we're tucked into bed. It's as if God is saying, "Rest up, I've got this. And guess what? Tomorrow, we get to do it all over again, you and me, as partners."

There's a beautiful power in letting go and just resting in God's peace. That may be the holiest kind of hustle!

I'm telling you, it's like spiritual self-care for your soul. The faith it takes to run your race is the same faith it takes to rest. You can be confident that even as you lay down in peace, as Psalm 4:8 beautifully puts it, God's up, running things just fine.

So, let's make a pact tonight: give yourself grace for what you didn't get to, thank God for what you did, and let Him take care of the rest.

Sleep with a heart full of peace, and wake up with a spirit ready to take on the world again. Are you in?

"In peace I will lie down and sleep, for you alone, Lord, make me dwell in safety."
Psalm 4:8 NIV

How does intention become action?

Alright, let's get into it. We're talking about the "I" word—Intention. It's one thing to have good intentions, and another thing to actually put wheels on them. I'm a huge fan of that verse in Luke 14:28, where it talks about counting the cost before diving into a project. It's like Life 101!

At the end of each day take a moment to pause, breathe, and think about tomorrow. I know you're tired, but hey, we all need some 'me time' to figure out what's most important for the next day. It's about aim and alignment. You've got to know your target.

So you want to exercise tomorrow? Cool, set the intention, but don't stop there. Set your alarm, lay out those running shoes and yoga pants so they're the first thing you see when you wake up. Make it hard to say no!

Or maybe you're the person who loves to hit snooze? No judgment here, but if you want to break that habit, set your intention, and then put that alarm clock on the other side of the room. Make it so you have to physically get up to turn it off.

This is your shot to clear the fog and zoom in on what matters most. It's like setting the GPS for your day. You wouldn't start a road trip without setting your destination, would you?

This isn't about wishful thinking; it's about wishful doing.

You set the intention, you make the plan, and then you lay out the steps to get there. That's how dreams turn into reality, how goals get met, and how you become the you that you've always wanted to be.

So tonight, get clear. Set your intention for tomorrow, lay out your plans, and set yourself up for success. Write down one intention followed by 2 action steps that will prepare the way, remove the obstacles, and set you up to follow through tomorrow!

"But don't begin until you count the cost. For who would begin construction of a building without first calculating the cost to see if there is enough money to finish it?"
Luke 14:28 NLT

How can Thanksgiving transform your tomorrow?

Alright, let's dive into something that can transform your everyday life—Thanksgiving, and I don't mean the holiday with turkey and dressing. We're talking about the gritty kind of gratitude, God's way. 1 Thessalonians 5:16-18 tells us to "rejoice always, pray continually, give thanks in all circumstances." It's not a suggestion; it's a divine nudge!

What do you do to wind down at the end of your day? That is the perfect moment to whip out that journal or take mental stock. Let's get gritty with our gratitude. What made you laugh today? Jot it down!

You see, the joyous moments, no matter how small, are hints of God's goodness sprinkled into your day.

Now, think about your wins for the day. What are you proud of? Don't overlook this step; give yourself some credit. Our victories, whether big or small, are worth celebrating. Yes, you heard me, celebrate YOU!

Oh, let's not forget those unexpected blessings—those moments that caught you off guard in the best way possible.

God loves to surprise us, doesn't He? Let's cherish and thank Him for those.

How about opportunities for growth? Yeah, even those uncomfortable, cringe-worthy situations have a silver lining. Thank God for them because they're essentially the gym equipment for your soul. You're getting spiritually ripped, my friend!

Now, why does this thanksgiving practice feel so small sometimes? Probably because it's so easy to do and it's just as easy NOT to do. But let me tell you, there's dynamite power in this habit. It can blow up your stress and pave the way for a peaceful sleep. So don't just slide into bed tonight without taking your spiritual grit to the next level.

Seal your day with thanksgiving. You won't regret it!

"Give thanks in all circumstances; for this is the will of God in Christ Jesus for you."
1 Thessalonians 5:18 ESV

What Are You Aiming to Perfect Today?

Let's get real for a moment—nobody gets it right on the first try, or even the second. If you've stepped into this journey thinking you're going to nail it perfectly from day one, let me disrupt that notion.

Real grit isn't handed out at birth or a trait buried in your DNA; it's a decision you make every single day.

It's choosing to keep going when you'd rather not, embracing the mess and the chaos as if they were stepping stones to your divine destiny.

If you're hoping for a life well-lived, forget perfection!

Why? Because oftentimes, it's during the pursuit of what's good, what's divine, that we find the richest growth. When you're waist-deep in challenges, you're not failing, you're *fermenting*, marinating in the spices of life that will bring out your richest flavors.

So if you stumble, start again—and again, and again. The key is to keep at it until you discover what makes your soul sing.

Are you a pen and paper person? Or do you find liberation in tapping away at a keyboard? Both paths are worthy, because it's less about the method and more about the intentionality of the practice. For some of you, it's not even writing—it's meditating and visualizing a life so vivid you can almost touch it.

If some of these concepts are new to you, don't wait to be ready to start! Just start!

Perfection is not the goal here; growth is. Every tiny step forward is a win. If this is a new rhythm for you, set up a cue to help you remember. Maybe it's an alarm or maybe you have a journal smack-dab in the middle of your nightstand as your cue for the new. Rise ten minutes earlier than the world demands; it's a small sacrifice for a larger gain.

Do not despise these small beginnings, for the LORD rejoices to see the work begin, to see the plumb line in Zerubbabel's hand."
Zechariah 4:10 NLT

BONUS

Heather created a 90-day journal for you to develop GRIT God's Way!

Days 82-90 were a small snippet of what you will find outlined in this powerful guided journal experience!

Establish a structured a.m. and p.m. routine to create and establish biblical mindsets, habits, and disciplines that will enable you to win each day!

Scan the QR code below to get your copy today!

BONUS

To connect with Heather Wallace and discover more of her content visit her website at

www.heatherannwallace.com

Or scan the QR code below.

Heather is also available for speaking engagements and booking information can be located on her website.

Made in the USA
Monee, IL
15 February 2024